EDITOR: MARTIN WINDROW

OSPREY MILITARY MEN-AT-ARMS SERIES 92

INDIAN INFANTRY REGIMENTS 1860-1914

W9-ACJ-543

Text by
MICHAEL BARTHORP
Colour plates by
JEFFREY BURN

Published in 1979 by
Osprey Publishing Ltd
59 Grosvenor Street, London, W1X 9DA
© Copyright 1979 Osprey Publishing Ltd
Reprinted 1992

ISBN 0 85045 307 0

Filmset by BAS Printers Limited,
Over Wallop, Hampshire
Printed in Hong Kong

In preparing this book an invaluable source has been
the *Notes on the Armies of India*, compiled and published
by the Marquess of Cambridge in the Journal of the
Society for Army Historical Research, Volumes
XLVII–XLVIII. Other works which have proved
useful and which can be recommended to readers who
wish to study the subject in greater depth than can be
attempted here are: G. F. Macmunn and A. C.
Lovett, *Armies of India* (1911), Donovan Jackson,
India's Armies (1942), W. Y. Carman, *Indian Army
Uniforms—Infantry* (1969), T. A. Heathcote, *The Indian
Army* (1974), and Philip Mason, *A Matter of Honour*
(1974).
   The author is grateful to Miss J. M. Spencer-Smith
and Mr A. F. H. Bowden of the National Army
Museum for their help over various points, and
is also greatly indebted to Mr R. G. Harris for his
ever-friendly advice, knowledge and assistance during
the compilation of the work and for making available
numerous photographs from his extensive collection.

Introduction

Immediately prior to the Indian Mutiny of 1857–59 the Government of British India, which stretched from Sind and the Punjab in the west to Burma in the east, was exercised by the East India Company, whose activities were supervised by a Board of Control in London. The country was divided into three Presidencies—Bengal, Madras and Bombay. After the Mutiny the Company's rule was abolished and thereafter India was governed directly by the Crown with, in London, a Secretary of State for India and his department, the India Office. Responsible to the Secretary of State was the Governor-General, who was also Governor of Bengal and increasingly known as the Viceroy of India. Madras and Bombay each had their own Governors who were responsible for the affairs of their own Presidencies, but were subordinate to the Governor-General in matters affecting India as a whole.

Under the Company's rule each Presidency had its own army under its own commander-in-chief; however, the head of the Bengal Army was also C-in-C India, and as such exercised general control over the Madras and Bombay Armies. After the Mutiny, which was almost entirely confined to the Bengal Army, this arrangement continued. Outside the C-in-C's control was the Punjab Irregular (later Frontier) Force, a collection of regiments of cavalry and infantry, technically belonging to the Bengal Army, whose task was the security of the North-West Frontier. This force was controlled by the Lieutenant-Governor of the Punjab until 1886, when it was brought under the C-in-C's control as part of the Bengal Army proper, though retaining its identity as a separate force within that army.

In 1895 the three Presidency armies were abolished in favour of four Commands: the Punjab (including the Frontier Force), Bengal, Madras (including Burma) and Bombay (including Sind and Baluchistan). Each Command was under a lieutenant-general who was responsible to the C-in-C India. The regiments, however, continued to bear their old Presidency names and numbers. When Lord Kitchener was appointed C-in-C India in 1902 he undertook a major reorganization of the entire army in India, in the course of which all vestiges of the old Presidency armies disappeared. Henceforth there was to be one Indian Army, and to emphasize this all regiments were re-designated and numbered in one sequence throughout. This system remained in force up to the outbreak of the Great War, and thereafter until the next reorganization in 1922.

The purpose of this book is to examine the infantry regiments of the Indian Army between

Sepoy, havildar and Indian officer, 4th Infantry, Punjab Irregular Force, in early drab uniform, *c.* 1860. Note the native sword (*tulwar*) and shield of the officer. The men are, from left to right, an Afridi, a Sikh and an Afghan. Lithograph by Captain W. Fane. (National Army Museum)

Indian regiments that took part in the Egyptian War of 1882. The infantry figures are, from *1st left*: 7th Bengal N.I., officer; (*3rd*) 20th Punjab Infantry, sepoy; (*4th*) 29th Bombay N.I. (2nd Baluch), British officer; (*8th*) 20th Punjab, officer; (*9th*) 7th Bengal, sepoy; (*10th, 12th*) 29th (2nd Baluch), officer and naik. After a watercolour by Orlando Norie. (Collections R. G. Harris)

1860–1914. In view of their number, this can only be done in broad terms, and with the individual regiment's changes of designation, dress distinctions and battle honours set out in tabulated form.

The Gurkha regiments, which formed a highly distinguished and sizeable element of the Indian infantry, have already been the subject of a volume in this series; therefore they will only be referred to in the text in places where their omission would leave an incomplete picture of the Indian infantry as a whole.

Organization

Prior to the Mutiny the Bengal Army had seventy-four regular native infantry regiments, Madras fifty-two and Bombay twenty-nine. Each army's regiments were numbered in sequence according to the 1824 reorganization of the Company's forces.

In addition there were several 'irregular' battalions, such as those in the Punjab Irregular Force, and local troops. During the Mutiny sixty-four of the Bengal regiments mutinied or were disarmed, but, with the exception of partial disaffection in two Bombay regiments, the infantry of the other two Presidencies remained loyal. The troops of the Punjab Irregular Force also proved steadfast and, together with new regiments raised in the Punjab, played a major part in assisting British regiments to suppress the mutineers.

In the reorganization that followed, all the Bengal regiments were re-numbered and, since none of the disloyal regiments were retained, the senior loyal regiment, the 21st, became the 1st Bengal Native Infantry; the next, formerly the 31st, became the 2nd, and so on. Some regiments which had merely been disarmed as a precautionary measure were re-admitted. These, plus various Sikh and Gurkha battalions, together with the new regiments raised in the Punjab during the Mutiny and some other battalions formed from loyal elements of mutinous regiments, were all taken into the Bengal Line which, under the first reorganization of May 1861, numbered forty-eight regiments. In October 1861 it was decided to renumber the four existing Gurkha units separately, so all regiments junior to them moved up in seniority. Thus the new Bengal Line comprised the 1st–44th, joined, in 1864, by the 45th, converted from a Sikh police battalion, better known as Rattray's Sikhs. The infantry composition of the Punjab Frontier Force was regularized in 1865 at four regiments of Sikh infantry, six of Punjabis, one Gurkha regiment (the 5th), and the infantry element of the Corps of Guides.

In the Madras Army no reorganization was required and the regiments continued under the 1824 designations; but only briefly, for between 1862 and 1864 the eleven regiments numbered 42nd–52nd were disbanded. The 21st, 27th and 29th Bombay Native Infantry were disbanded between 1858 and 1860, their places in the Bombay Line being taken by a Marine battalion and two Baluch battalions, while a third such battalion, raised in 1858, completed the Bombay infantry as the 30th. Thus, by 1865, the infantry of the Bengal Army numbered forty-five regiments, four of Gurkha Rifles, and one, un-numbered, Bhopal battalion; the Punjab Frontier Force had eleven, including one of Gurkhas; Madras had forty-one and Bombay thirty.

Some of these regiments had the honorary titles of 'grenadiers', 'light infantry' or 'rifles', but none bore the designation 'fusiliers' as this had been reserved for the senior of the Company's European regiments which, in 1860, were taken with the other Europeans into the British Line as 101st–109th Foot, though retaining their old names of Bengal, Madras or Bombay. Thus, for example, the 1st European Bengal Fusiliers became the 101st Royal Bengal Fusiliers, and later, in 1881, 1st Battalion Royal Munster Fusiliers (disbanded in 1922). Two of the Bengal regiments, the 23rd and 32nd, were designated 'Pioneers'. These had been raised in the Punjab during the Mutiny for pioneering tasks in areas where local civilians were untrustworthy, and were afterwards taken into the Bengal Line as units able to undertake normal infantry, as well as pioneering, duties. Subsequently other pioneer regiments were raised or converted in all three armies.

After the Second Afghan War of 1878–80 the establishments of all three armies were reduced, and in 1882 a number of regiments were disban-

Officers and men, 1st Infantry, Punjab Irregular Force, c. 1860. Note the poshteen coat of the right-hand officer. See notes to colour plate A3. Lithograph by Captain W. Fane. (National Army Museum)

British and Indian officers, havildars, drummers and Colours of the 8th Bengal Native Infantry, c. 1870. The British officers are wearing the 1856 British pattern tunic, the Indian ranks the first 'Zouave' pattern, introduced for the Bengal Army from 1863. All have black trousers with a red welt. (Collection R. G. Harris)

Right:
British and Indian officers, 26th (Punjab) Regiment, Bengal Native Infantry, 1873, in full dress drab tunics of Rifles pattern, worn by Punjab and Frontier Force regiments. The dark tunic belongs to the Surgeon. (Collection R. G. Harris)

ded: the 34th–37th and 41st Bengal Infantry, the 3rd Infantry Punjab Frontier Force, the 30th–41st Madras Infantry, and the 6th, 11th, 15th and 18th Bombay Infantry—twenty-one in all. Eight years later the 39th Bengal and the 10th Madras were disbanded. However, following the Anglo-Russian crisis of 1885, when a Russian invasion of India was feared, four new Bengal regiments were raised in 1887 and took the vacant numbers of 34–37, while a second battalion raised for the 3rd Gurkhas at the same time was converted in 1890 into the 39th Bengal Infantry, later Garhwal Rifles. From 1885 the word 'Native', which had acquired undesirable connotations, was dropped from the titles of all regiments. Between 1900–01 four more regiments were added to the Bengal Infantry, the senior taking the vacant number of 41, and in 1902 the 8th Gurkha Rifles was raised. The 8th Madras In-

fantry, briefly designated 8th Gurkhas, was disbanded the same year.

Thus, immediately prior to the Kitchener reforms of 1903, the regiments of the four Commands were as follows:

Bengal: 1st–48th (including four of Pioneers and four—9th, 42nd, 43rd and 44th—of Gurkhas). 1st–4th Gurkha Rifles.
Two un-numbered battalions—Bhopal and Mharwara.

Sepoy, 2nd Bengal Native Light Infantry in 'Zouave' tunic, c. 1875. Although turbans had been approved in 1860 to replace the Kilmarnock cap, worn here, the 2nd were still wearing the latter in the 1880s. The loose trousers, worn here with bare legs instead of white gaiters, replaced the straight type in 1869. (Collection R. G. Harris)

Madras: 1st–33rd (including three of Pioneers).

Bombay: 1st–5th, 7th–10th, 12th–14th, 16th, 17th, 19th–30th (including two of Pioneers).

Punjab: 1st–4th Sikh Infantry.
1st, 2nd, 4th–6th Punjab Infantry.
5th Gurkha Rifles.
Guides Infantry.

As each of these regiments had only one battalion, with the exception of the 1st–5th Gurkhas and the 39th Garhwal Rifles, which each had two, there

were in Bengal fifty-eight battalions, in Madras thirty-three, in Bombay twenty-six, and in the Punjab eleven, making one hundred and twenty-nine battalions in all.

Hitherto the Indian regiments had been localized in their own regions, scattered all over the sub-continent with the main task of ensuring the internal security of India. There had been exceptions in major campaigns as when some Madras Pioneers served in the Second Afghan War; a few Bengal regiments were used in the Third Burma War of 1885–87, and on expeditions outside India. Since the Mutiny, however, there had been no civil insurrection and the pacification of the North-West Frontier had been within the capacity of the Bengal and Punjab troops, aided by British battalions and with some help from Bombay. Kitchener considered that the internal security rôle was quite secondary to what he saw as the main threat, the possibility of a Russian invasion from the north-west, and that the chief rôle of the army in India was the defence of that frontier. To that end, the bulk of the army should be stationed within reach of the threatened zone, in Sind and the Punjab. The localization of regiments was abolished, and in future every regiment was to have the opportunity of experiencing frontier conditions. To underline this policy, it was important that each regiment felt itself part of the Indian Army as a whole and not solely concerned with its own Command. A divisional and brigade command system was instituted, and a new method of numbering and designating regiments was introduced. The new titles can be found in a later section, but the re-numbering went as follows. Bengal regiments retained their existing numbers. The Punjab regiments, less the 5th Gurkhas, were numbered consecutively, adding 50, so that, for example, the 4th Sikh Infantry and the 1st Punjab Infantry became 54th and 55th. The Guides remained unnumbered. Madras regiments added 60 and, since over the years a number of them had been increasingly recruited in the Punjab, this was recognized in their titles, the 30th Madras, for example, becoming the 90th Punjabis. The Hyderabad Contingent regiments were brought into the Line as 94th–99th. The Bombay regiments added 100, so that the 1st Bombay Grenadiers became the 101st Grenadiers, and so on. The first five Gurkha regiments remained as before and were joined by the other five Gurkha corps from the Bengal Line and the 10th from Madras, after a somewhat involved renumbering, thus:

1901	1903	1907
8th GR	2/10th GR	7th GR
		(Two bns.)
9th GR	9th GR	(Two bns.)
42nd BI	6th GR	(Two bns.)
43rd BI	7th GR	2/8 GR
44th BI	8th GR	1/8 GR
10th MI	1/10th GR	(Two bns.)

Apart from another regiment of Pioneers raised in 1904, which took the number left vacant by the disbanded (in 1882) 6th Bombay Infantry, thus becoming the 106th, this remained the order of battle of the Indian infantry up to and throughout the early years of the Great War. In 1922 another major reorganization took place in which the existing regiments became battalions of large regiments, each of four battalions and a training battalion, e.g. the 25th, 26th, 27th, 28th and 29th Punjabis became the 1st, 2nd, 3rd, 4th and 10th Battalions, The 15th Punjab Regiment.

As already mentioned, each regiment, with the exception of the Gurkha and Garhwal Rifles, had only one battalion. From 1860 this was divided into eight companies, each under an Indian officer, a *subadar*, with a *jemadar* as second-in-command, and consisting of five *havildars* (sergeants), five *naiks* (corporals), two drummers and seventy-five *sepoys*. Four companies formed a wing, each under a British officer, and at battalion headquarters was the commandant, second-in-command, adjutant, quartermaster, medical officer and one general duties officer, all British, making eight British officers per battalion. From 1866 a senior Indian officer, the *subadar-major*, was added to battalion headquarters. Experience in the Second Afghan War proved that the establishment of British officers was too small to allow for casualties, and thereafter each wing commander received a British subaltern as second-in-command.

In the 1890s the eight-company organization was changed to one of four double-companies, each commanded by a British major or captain, with a captain or subaltern as second-in-command, and sometimes with young officers under training

Sepoys Dewa Singh and Dehan Singh of the 3rd Sikh Infantry, Punjab Frontier Force, orderlies to General Roberts during the Second Afghan War, 1878–80. They have Snider rifles and pouch-belt equipment. Watercolour by Colonel G. R. Woodthorpe, R.E. (National Army Museum).

attached. The double-company contained four half-companies, two commanded by subadars and two by jemadars, each consisting of two havildars and forty sepoys split into two sections. By 1914, therefore, though the number of Indian officers had remained constant, the total of British had nearly doubled since the 1860s.

Officers and Men

Under the Company, regular infantry battalions had a much higher proportion of British officers, over twenty, although irregular units made do with three. Unlike the British Army, where officers obtained the Queen's Commission and further promotion by the purchase system, Company officers, who tended to come from less affluent backgrounds, studied at the Company's Military

Seminary at Addiscombe for a two-year course, after which they were commissioned in one of the native (or European) regiments. This commission was granted in the name of the Crown but held no validity west of the Cape of Good Hope. Thereafter promotion went entirely by regimental seniority, which meant that unless a regiment suffered heavy casualties in action or from disease, promotion was extremely slow; it took nearly thirty years to reach the rank of major, and field officers' ages ranged from the late forties to sixties. Unless they could find employment outside their regiments, either in the more interesting and better paid irregular corps, on the staff, or in political appointments, Company officers stagnated in their regiments with consequent loss of efficiency. The deficiencies of this system were highlighted by the sudden shock of the Mutiny.

When the Company's armies were transferred to the Crown, officers for Indian regiments were trained at the Royal Military College, Sandhurst, from which, providing they passed out among the top thirty cadets of any one term, they were granted the same Queen's Commission as British Army officers, although the latter always took precedence over officers of equivalent rank in the Indian service. In order to iron out the anomalies of promotion by regimental seniority, cadets were commissioned, not to individual regiments, but to a pool of officers in whichever Presidency they were destined for, known as the Bengal, Madras or Bombay Staff Corps. All appointments, whether to civil posts, headquarters staffs or to regiments, were filled from these Staff Corps, which in 1891 were amalgamated into one Indian Staff Corps; after 1903 officers were simply commissioned into the 'Indian Army'. Promotion was henceforth by length of service, not regimental seniority, with lieutenants being promoted to captain after eleven years, captains to major after twenty, majors to lieutenant-colonel after twenty-six, and lieutenant-colonels to colonel after thirty-one years. Nevertheless, this was still slow progress up the rank structure, and its inevitability did nothing to encourage initiative. Furthermore, in the 1860s and 1870s, there were still many officers who were too old for their work; and once an officer had achieved command of his regiment there was little to prevent him hanging on to it for as long as he wished. This particularly applied in the Bombay and Madras Armies, where casualties had been light in the Mutiny compared to the Bengal Army. After the Second Afghan War it was ruled that commanding officers then in post, and their immediate successors, should give up command after seven years tenure or on reaching the age of 55; thereafter the age limit for regimental com-

45th (Rattray's Sikh) Regiment, Bengal Native Infantry with prisoners during the Second Afghan War. See colour plate D1 and notes. (National Army Museum)

mand was to be 52. Even so, this was fairly elderly for a campaign on the North-West Frontier.

About half the British officers going into Indian regiments had family connections, often extensive, with India. Most came from legal, clerical, medical or service families, the professional middle class, rather than from the aristocracy and landed gentry which officered the British Army. In the period 1890–95, twenty-seven officers commissioned into the British Army were the sons of titled men but only one such entered the Indian Staff Corps. Many were men of high calibre and often professionally more dedicated than their British counterparts; but the slow promotion, their dependence, in default of private means, on their pay and subsequent pension, the long years spent in a destructive climate, all tended to make for an elderly officer type in the higher ranks, who had lost the drive and enthusiasm of his youth.

Whatever the defects of the system, there can be no doubt that most British officers established a tremendous bond with their sepoys, and the mutual trust and respect between officers and men of vastly different cultures proved strong enough to overcome the memories of the Mutiny, and ultimately to hold together in the conditions of modern European warfare of 1914–18.

Until after the Great War no Indian could receive the Sovereign's Commission granted to their British officers. Indian soldiers could be promoted from the non-commissioned ranks to jemadar, subadar and subadar-major, receiving a commission from the Viceroy. They were then theoretically in command of half-companies and companies. However, their disciplinary powers were limited; they were sometimes, by virtue of long service spent in the ranks, too old to exercise the duties carried out in British regiments by subalterns; and though they were loyal, brave and devoted soldiers, they tended to lack the education and leadership qualities required for the satisfactory conduct of their commands, particularly as warfare became more technical. Their position in a company of infantry was thus more comparable to that of a British company-sergeant-major than a company or platoon commander, such duties falling more within the province of the British officers. On the other hand, they provided an invaluable link between the British officer (es-

Band Havildar, 1st Sikh Infantry, Frontier Force, 1880, in full dress drab tunic. Although the facings appear dark, they were in fact yellow. (Collection R. G. Harris)

pecially when he was new to India) and the sepoys of the company, advising the former on the latter's customs, foibles, religious habits, diet, strengths and weaknesses.

Before the Mutiny the Bengal regiments were very largely composed of high-caste Hindu sepoys, Brahmans and Rajputs from Oudh and Behar. These were tall, relatively fair-skinned men, usually the sons of small land-owners and tenant-farmers, generally thought to be more desirable as soldiers than the smaller, darker, lower-caste men to be found in the Madras and Bombay Armies. In the latter two forces, men of all castes soldiered side by side, whereas in Bengal the privileges and prohibitions of the caste system were afforded every consideration by the authorities. A Madras subadar said, 'We put our religion in our knapsacks when our colours are unfurled'; and a Bengal sepoy, who transferred to the Bombay Army after a man of lower caste was promoted over him, pointed out that in Bengal men took pride in their caste but in Bombay their pride was in their regiment. These differences go far to explaining why, when fears about their religion and increasing distrust of their officers drove the Bengal regiments to mutiny, the other two armies were almost completely unaffected.

The Mutiny could not have been quelled by British troops alone had it not been for the aid of the Bombay and Madras Armies, the few faithful Bengal regiments, the Gurkha regiments, and new battalions of Sikhs and Muslims raised in the Punjab and of Baluchis and Pathans from the frontier regions. When the time came to reconstruct the armies of India, it was these men from the north-west and the Gurkhas, the 'martial races' as they were known, who became the favourite source for recruiters. They had proved their worth as foes in the first half of the century and as allies in the Mutiny, they took naturally to soldiering, and they were even more imposing in appearance than the old Bengal sepoys.

As the century progressed, it was on the North-West Frontier that the services of Indian regiments were increasingly required. The prevailing view of British officers, led by Lord Roberts, was that it was only the Sikhs, Dogras, Jats, Punjabi Mussulmans, Gurkhas, Afridis and so on of the northern races who were hardy and tough enough, not only for frontier warfare against the turbulent tribes of Afghanistan, but also, as the Russian threat to India loomed larger, to face a European enemy. Hence recruiting became more and more confined to these races, both in the Bengal and Bombay Armies and also in Madras where, since the inhabitants of southern India no longer found favour as soldiers (except as sappers), regiments were either disbanded or simply recruited from the Punjab, eventually changing their designations to reflect their new composition.

Since the value of mixing men of all castes and classes in the Madras and Bombay Armies had been proved in the Mutiny, a committee set up in 1858 recommended that such a policy should be followed in all three Presidencies. In the Bengal Army this happened in some regiments, but the trend was increasingly towards either the 'class-company' system, in which the men of each company were homogeneous, or the 'class-regiment', the latter becoming more popular as the century progressed. For example, the 16th BNI in 1864 was a mixed regiment of Hindustani Muslims, Brahmans and Rajputs, Ahirs, Sikhs and some low-caste men. By 1884 it had become a class-company regiment, with two companies of Hindustani Muslims, one of Brahmans, three of Rajputs, and two of other Hindus. In 1892 it was entirely composed of

2nd Bengal Light Infantry clearing a village near Minhla, Third Burma War, 1885–87. Note the Kilmarnocks still being worn. Engraving from the *Illustrated London News* 1886. (Collection R. G. Harris)

Indian officer and men of the 45th (Rattray's Sikh) Regiment at the Delhi Camp of Exercise, 1886. All ranks are wearing khaki kurtas (blouses), trousers and puttees with brown leather equipment as for field service. (Collection R. G. Harris)

Rajputs. By that date the Bengal infantry consisted of thirty class regiments, seven of Sikhs, eight of Gurkhas, two Brahman, seven Rajput, four Hindustani Muslim, two Jat; and eighteen class-company regiments, mainly Punjabi Muslims (usually called Mussulmans), Punjabi Hindus (Sikhs, Jats, Dogras) and some Afridis. This trend was followed by the smaller Presidencies: in Bombay with regiments of Mahrattas, Rajputs and Baluchis, and in Madras, as already mentioned with Punjabis. The Frontier Force regiments were all Sikhs, Punjabis, Gurkhas and hillmen such as Afridis, Pathans and Khuttucks.

All soldiers were long-service volunteers. They joined for pay and security, for the uniform, for the chance of fame, for the privilege of bearing arms, or to continue a family or class tradition of military service. The sepoy served not for any patriotic motive, of which there was none (unlike in the present Indian Army), but to establish and preserve his own honour so that he stood well in the eyes of his family and community, and for the honour of his company and his regiment. Providing his officers cared for, trusted and respected him, he gave them, and through them his regiment, loyalty and steadfastness.

After forty years' service, or twenty-one from 1886, he received a pension, either in cash or as a grant of land. Indian officers were rewarded for loyal service with the Order of British India, which included a pay increase, and, since Indian soldiers were ineligible for the Victoria Cross until 1912, acts of conspicuous gallantry were recognized by the award of the Indian Order of Merit, which also brought an increase of pay and pension.

On Campaign

In the period under review Indian regiments served in several expeditions outside India: to China in 1860, Abyssinia in 1868, Egypt in 1882, the Sudan and Burma in 1885, China again in 1900, Somaliland in 1903, Tibet in 1904, culminating in the despatch of the Indian Corps to France in 1914. Their chief theatre of operations was Afghanistan and the North-West Frontier, where regiments were almost constantly on active service, ranging from minor skirmishing to major outbreaks of trouble like the Umbeyla expedition of 1863, the Black Mountain operations of 1881 and 1891, the siege and relief of Chitral in 1895, the Tirah and Malakand expeditions in 1897, operations against the Mohmands and Zakka Khel in 1908, and one full-scale campaign against regular troops, the Second Afghan War of 1878–80. There is not space here to go into the details of these campaigns, or the

parts played by regiments involved in them, although individual regiments' participation in the more important ones can be gleaned from their battle honours, which appear in a later section. However, some examples can be given to demonstrate the quality of Indian troops in the field.

In March 1879 a detachment of the 45th Sikhs under Lieutenant Barclay was providing a protective escort for Captain Leach, Royal Engineers, who was carrying out a survey reconnaissance, when they were attacked on a hill by large numbers of Shinwari tribesmen. The party began an orderly withdrawal, one half covering the other, but, as the Shinwaris advanced firing, Barclay was hit. Some of his Sikhs started to carry him downhill while Leach organized a skirmishing line to protect the retreat. As the tribesmen closed in for a rush, Leach called the troops together and led them in a sudden bayonet charge to forestall it. After a fierce fight he was able to continue the withdrawal, although the outnumbered Sikhs had to charge twice more before Barclay could be got away. Leach was awarded the v.c. for his leadership, but the Sikhs' gallant conduct in the face of superior numbers was

Left:
Colour-Havildar, 11th Bengal Infantry, 1887. A Brahman of Oudh, the type that predominated in the pre-Mutiny Bengal Army. Note the Kilmarnock also retained by this regiment and the brown leather equipment introduced *c.* 1880. (National Army Museum)
Centre:
Subadar, 18th Bengal Infantry, 1887. The crossed swords denoting his rank can be seen below the collar on his right side. Note the cut-away central panel of the tunic, and puttees instead of white gaiters. (National Army Museum)
Right:
A Pathan sepoy, 20th (Punjab) Regiment, Bengal Infantry, 1887. Drab-uniformed regiments did not have the central panel to their tunics. Note also the cotton, not cloth, trousers, the canvas gaiters and native shoes. (National Army Museum)

also undoubtedly inspired by their determination to try to save their wounded officer.

One of the finest and most experienced of the Frontier Force regiments was the Guides. A detachment had provided the escort for the British Resident at Kabul in 1879. When the Residency was attacked and their single British officer killed, they fought and died to the last man, despite being offered safe conduct by the Afghans. Later that year the Guides made an epic march in the depths of winter, through mountainous and hostile country, to reach Roberts' small force besieged by 100,000 Afghans in the Sherpur cantonment near Kabul.

The maxim followed by the Guides in frontier warfare was: 'Be fiery quick in attack, but deadly slow in retirement.' The latter they demonstrated in masterly fashion during the advance of General Low's force to relieve the fort of Chitral in 1895. On reaching the Panjkora River the Guides Infantry was sent across first, to establish a bridgehead and clear the neighbourhood of any enemy who might resist the crossing of the main body next day. During the night the river rose fourteen feet and the bridge was swept away, leaving the Guides isolated. They nevertheless continued to clear the high ground in front of the bridgehead with five companies, but while they were doing so some 8,000 tribesmen appeared, some attacking the Guides while others moved to cut off their line of retreat. Despite their danger the Guides fell back slowly, one company covering the other, their cool demeanour and accurate musketry holding off the enemy horde until they were within covering fire from the main body. The bridgehead was reached in safety, but in the closing stages of the withdrawal the commanding officer, Colonel Fred Battye, was killed. Seeing him fall, the Afridi company turned without orders and made a fierce counter-attack with the bayonet to avenge his death. Low's column eventually reached Chitral, which had been defended for forty-six days by a company of the 14th Sikhs and some irregular Kashmiri Levies, only to find that it had already been relieved by a smaller column from the north led by Colonel Kelly and mainly consisting of the 32nd Pioneers. Kelly's men had fought their way for nearly a month over 220 miles of snow-covered mountains and raging torrents.

It would be futile to pretend that all Indian regiments behaved impeccably in action. During Roberts' night approach march against the Afghan defences on the Peiwar Kotal in the early stages of the Second Afghan War, the reliability of some of the Pathan elements of his leading regiment, the 29th Punjab Infantry, suddenly became suspect and Roberts hurriedly had to place the 5th Gurkhas in front to save surprise being lost. At the disaster of Maiwand in 1880, two companies of the 30th Bombay Infantry fled, their panic infecting the rest of their regiment and the hitherto steady 1st Bombay Grenadiers, leaving the British 66th Foot without support. It must be said, however, that the men who broke were mostly young Pathan recruits; their single British officer, who was young and inexperienced, had been killed, and their Indian officers, who had had little control over them, had been wounded.

Lord Roberts held the view that however brave Indian officers and men were, they always looked to the British officer in times of difficulty and danger. This was an unfair generalization, as can be seen from the action of Subadar Sayad Ahmed Shah and twenty-five men of the 31st Punjab Infantry in the Malakand expedition of 1897. They held out in a small post against repeated attacks by fanatical tribesmen, losing nineteen men killed and wounded, and only withdrawing, carrying their wounded, when the post was set on fire. The subadar himself was wounded but continued to direct the defence, receiving the Order of Merit for his gallantry. Earlier in the year a treacherous attack was made by tribesmen in the Tochi Valley on a political officer who was escorted by a small party of the 1st Sikhs and 1st Punjabis of the Frontier Force. The British officers were all killed or wounded, but a steady and disciplined retreat was carried out under the command of the Indian officers, Subadar Sundar Singh and twelve men of the 1st Punjabis sacrificing their lives to enable the rest to get clear.

The 36th Sikhs were the only regiment to bear the battle honour 'Samana', awarded for the defence of Fort Gulistan in the Tirah in 1897 by two companies. The fort also had a detached post at Saraghari, a blockhouse made of mud bricks set up on the crest of the Samana range to facilitate heliograph communications between Gulistan and Fort Lockhart. This was held by a detachment of nineteen men of the same regiment and two cook-boys. On 12 September the post was attacked by several thousand Orakzais. For six and a half hours the tiny group of Sikhs fought off continued attacks until their last man was killed and the post overrun.

It was a far cry from the Frontier to the rain-filled trenches of France in 1914, from facing tribesmen armed only with rifles to confronting the most powerful army in Europe. The first Indian regiment into action was the 129th Baluchis, who went into the line in late October and were soon involved in heavy fighting. On the 31st the Germans attacked and the battalion's two machine guns were cut off. The crews fought their guns until

only one man, Sepoy Khudadad Khan, was left alive. He was wounded and was left for dead by the Germans but eventually managed to crawl back and rejoin his regiment. He became the first Indian soldier to win the Victoria Cross.

The Regiments

The regiments are listed under the Army to which they belonged in 1860, i.e. Bengal, Madras and Bombay, and the Punjab Frontier Force according to its composition in 1865. Although most regiments received minor changes to their titles over the years, the system of numbering remained constant until the Kitchener reforms. The new numbers and titles will be found against the date '1903'.

Under each regiment is given its original date of formation and title; successive titles since 1860; the tunic and facing colour with subsequent changes; battle honours, those granted from 1860–1914 being in CAPITALS; and its designation in 1922, which may be more familiar to some readers.

Left:
Naik, 3rd Sikh Infantry, Frontier Force, 1887. A Jat Sikh, he wears a drab kurta with black facings and black puttees. The turban fringe is orange. (National Army Museum)

Centre:
A Hindu sepoy of Malabar, 1st Madras Infantry (Pioneers), 1887. The 'Zouave' tunic and loose trousers were introduced for the Madras Army in 1883, replacing the 1856 British tunic and straight trousers. (National Army Museum)

Right:
A Maratha Havildar, 5th Bombay Light Infantry, 1887, in the tunic/frock introduced with loose trousers and gaiters in 1880 to replace the 1856 British pattern; this frock was worn only by Bombay regiments. (National Army Museum)

BENGAL ARMY

The titles under which regiments first appear are those granted after the reorganization of the Bengal Army in May 1861.

1st Regiment of Bengal Native Infantry (BNI)
Raised 1776 as 30th Battalion. At Mutiny, 21st BNI.
1901: 1st Brahman Infantry. 1903: 1st Brahmans. Red; faced yellow, 1870 lemon yellow, 1886 white. Laswaree, Bhurtpore, BURMA 1885–87.
(4/1st Punjab Regt.)

2nd Bengal Light Infantry

Raised 1798 as 2/15th Regt. At Mutiny, 31st Light Infantry.

1876: 2nd (The Queen's Own) Bengal Native Light Infantry. 1897: 2nd (Queen's Own) Rajput Bengal Light Infantry. 1901: 2nd (Queen's Own) Rajput Light Infantry. 1911: 2nd Queen Victoria's Own Rajput Light Infantry.

Red; faced buff, 1879 blue.

Delhi, Laswaree, Deig, Bhurtpore, Khelat, Afghanistan, Maharajpore, Punjab, Chillianwallah, Goojerat, Central India, AFGHANISTAN 1879–80, BURMA 1885–87, CHINA 1900.

(1/7th Rajput Regt.)

3rd BNI

Raised 1798 as 1/16th. At Mutiny, 32nd.

1901: 3rd Brahman Infantry. 1903: 3rd Brahmans.

Red; faced black.

Bhurtpore, AFGHANISTAN 1879–80.

(Disbanded 1922)

4th BNI

Raised 1798 as 2/16th. At Mutiny, 33rd.

1890: 4th (Prince Albert Victor's) Bengal Infantry. 1897: 4th (Prince Albert Victor's) Rajput Regt., Bengal Infantry. 1901: 4th (Prince Albert Victor's) Rajput Infantry. 1903: 4th Prince Albert Victor's Rajputs.

Red; faced black.

Laswaree, Bhurtpore, Cabul 1842, Ferozeshah, Sobraon, AFGHANISTAN 1878–80, BURMA 1885–87.

(2/7th Rajput Regt.)

5th Bengal Light Infantry

Raised 1803 as 2/21st. At Mutiny, 42nd Light Infantry.

1903: 5th Light Infantry.

Red; faced yellow.

Arracan, Afghanistan, Kandahar, Ghuznee, Cabul 1842, Moodkee, Ferozeshah, Sobraon, AFGHANISTAN 1878–80, BURMA 1885–87.

(Disbanded 1922)

6th Bengal Light Infantry

Raised 1803 as 1/22nd. At Mutiny, 43rd Light Infantry.

1897: 6th Jat Regiment, Bengal Light Infantry. 1901: 6th Jat Light Infantry.

Red; faced pea-green, 1887 white.

Nagpore, Afghanistan, Kandahar 1842, Ghuznee, Cabul 1842, Maharajpore, Sobraon, ALI MASJID, AFGHANISTAN 1878–80, CHINA 1900.

(1/9th Jat Regt.)

7th BNI

Raised 1842 as 69th. At Mutiny, 47th.

1883: 7th (Duke of Connaught's Own) Regiment, BNI. 1893: 7th (Duke of Connaught's Own) Rajput Regiment of Bengal Infantry. 1903: 7th Duke of Connaught's Own Rajputs.

Red; faced yellow.

Moodkee, Ferozeshah, Aliwal, Sobraon, China 1858–59, EGYPT 1882, TEL-EL-KEBIR, PEKIN 1900.

(3/7th Rajput Regt.)

8th BNI

Raised 1814 as 1/30th. At Mutiny, 59th.

1897: 8th Rajput Regiment, Bengal Infantry.

Drum-Major, 7th Bombay Infantry in review order, c. 1890. Note the leather-reinforced white gaiters worn only by Bombay regiments. Dark blue pagri with red end and kulla. Watercolour by A. C. Lovett. (National Army Museum)

10th Madras Infantry in khaki crossing the Yaw River, Burma, 1889. Engraving from the Illustrated London News, 1889. (Collection R. G. Harris)

1901: 8th Rajput Infantry. 1903: 8th Rajputs.
Red; faced Saxon green, 1888 white, 1905 yellow.
Sobraon, AFGHANISTAN 1878–80.
(4/7th Rajput Regt.)

9th BNI
Raised 1817 as the Fatagarh Levy. At Mutiny, 63rd.
1894: 9th (Gurkha Rifle) Regiment, Bengal Infantry. 1901: 9th Gurkha Rifles. (Two battalions 1904.)
Red; faced yellow. 1894 Dark Green; faced black.
Bhurtpore, Sobraon, AFGHANISTAN 1878–80, PUNJAB FRONTIER.
(9th Gurkha Rifles)

Bhopal Levy
Raised 1859.
1865: The Bhopal Battalion. 1903: 9th Bhopal Infantry.
Drab; faced chocolate.
AFGHANISTAN 1878–80.
(4/16th Punjab Regt.)

10th BNI
Raised 1823 as 1/33rd. At Mutiny, 65th.
1897: 10th (Jat) Regiment, Bengal Infantry. 1901: 10th Jat Infantry. 1903: 10th Jats.
Red; faced yellow.
China 1858–59, BURMA 1885–87.
(3/9th Jat Regt.)

11th BNI
Raised 1815 as 1st Nasiri Battalion. At Mutiny, 66th or Gurkha Light Infantry.
1861 (Oct): 1st Gurkha Regiment Light Infantry.
1891: 1st Gurkha (Rifle) Regiment. (Two battalions from 1886.) 1901: 1st Gurkha Rifles. 1903: 1st Gurkha Rifles (The Malaun Regiment). 1906: 1st Prince of Wales's Own Gurkha Rifles (The Malaun Regiment). 1910: 1st King George's Own Gurkha Rifles (The Malaun Regiment)
Red; faced white. 1886, Rifle-Green; faced red.
Bhurtpore, Aliwal, Sobraon, AFGHANISTAN 1878–80, PUNJAB FRONTIER, TIRAH.
(1st K.G.O. Gurkha Rifles)

From October 1861, the four existing Gurkha regiments—11th, 17th, 18th, and 19th BNI—were taken out of the Bengal Line and numbered separately, so the regiments which had been numbered 12th–16th in May 1861 became the 11th–15th and the 20th–48th became the 16th–44th. The May number is given in brackets.

11th BNI (12th)
Raised 1825 as 2nd Extra Regiment. At Mutiny, 70th.
1897: 11th (Rajput) Regiment, Bengal Infantry.
1901: 11th Rajput Infantry. 1903: 11th Rajputs.

NCOs and sepoys of The Queen's Own Corps of Guides (Infantry), Frontier Force, in full dress drab tunics, faced red, 1890. The group includes men of most of the 'martial races' of India. The Sikh on the extreme right wears the Indian Order of Merit. (Collection Denis Quarmby)

Red; faced yellow.
Punjab, Chillianwallah, Goojerat, China 1858–59, AFGHANISTAN 1878–80, BURMA 1885–87.
(5/7th Rajput Regt.)

12th BNI (13th)
Raised 1838 as 3rd Regiment of Infantry, Shah Shujah's Force. At Mutiny, Regiment of Khelat-i-Gilzie.
1864: 12th (Khelat-i-Gilzie) Regiment, BNI. 1903: 12th Pioneers (Khelat-i-Gilzie Regiment).
Red; faced white, 1905 yellow, 1908 black.
Khelat-i-Gilzie, Kandahar, Ghuznee, Cabul 1842, Maharajpore, AFGHANISTAN 1878–80, BURMA 1885–87, PUNJAB FRONTIER.
(2nd Bn. Bombay Pioneers)

13th BNI (14th)
Raised 1835 as infantry of the Shekhawati Brigade. At Mutiny, the Shekhawati Battalion.
1884: 13th (Shekhawati Regiment) BNI. 1903: 13th Rajputs (The Shekhawati Regiment).
Red; faced blue, 1870 dark blue.
Aliwal, AFGHANISTAN 1878–80, CHITRAL.
(10/6th Rajputana Rifles)

14th BNI (15th)
Raised 1846 as the Regiment of Ferozepore.

1864: 14th (The Ferozepore) Regiment BNI. 1885: 14th BNI (Ferozepore Sikhs). 1901: 14th (Ferozepore) Sikh Infantry. 1903: 14th Ferozepore Sikhs. 1906: 14th Prince of Wales's Own Ferozepore Sikhs. 1910: 14th King George's Own Ferozepore Sikhs.
Red; faced yellow.
Lucknow, ALI MASJID, AFGHANISTAN 1878–79, DEFENCE OF CHITRAL, CHINA 1900.
(1/11th Sikh Regt.)

15th BNI (16th)
Raised 1846 as the Regiment of Ludhiana.
1864: 15th (Ludhiana) Regiment BNI. 1885: 15th BNI (Ludhiana Sikhs). 1901: 15th (Ludhiana) Sikh Infantry. 1903: 15th Ludhiana Sikhs.
Red; faced green, 1905 emerald green.
CHINA 1861–62, AHMED KHEL, KANDAHAR 1880, AFGHANISTAN 1878–80, SUAKIN 1885, TOFREK, CHITRAL, PUNJAB FRONTIER, TIRAH.
(2/11th Sikh Regt.)

2nd Gurkha Regiment (17th BNI)
Raised 1815 as the Sirmoor Battalion. At Mutiny, The Sirmoor Rifle Regiment.
1864: 2nd Goorkha (Sirmoor Rifle) Regiment. 1876: 2nd (Prince of Wales's Own) Goorkha Regiment (The Sirmoor Rifles). (Two battalions from 1886.) 1906: 2nd King Edward's Own Goorkha Rifles (The Sirmoor Regiment).
Green; faced and piped red, 1888 scarlet.
Bhurtpore, Aliwal, Sobraon, Delhi, KABUL 1879,

KANDAHAR 1880, AFGHANISTAN 1878–80, PUNJAB FRONTIER, TIRAH.
(2nd K.E.O. Goorkha Rifles)

3rd Gurkha Regiment (18th BNI)
Raised 1815 as the Kamaon Battalion. At Mutiny, 7th Kamaon Local Bn.
1864: 3rd (The Kamaon) Gurkha Regiment. 1887: 3rd Gurkha Regiment. 1891: 3rd Gurkha (Rifle) Regiment (Two battalions). 1901: 3rd Gurkha Rifles. 1907: 3rd The Queen's Own Gurkha Rifles. 1908: 3rd Queen Alexandra's Own Gurkha Rifles.
Green; faced black.
Delhi, AHMED KHEL, AFGHANISTAN 1878–80, BURMA 1885–87, CHITRAL, PUNJAB FRONTIER, TIRAH.
(3rd Gurkha Rifles)

Sepoys of the 16th Madras Infantry receiving a drink from a 'bhistie' during manoeuvres, 1889. Engraving after a photograph, *Illustrated London News*, 1891. (Collection R. G. Harris)

4th Gurkha Regiment (19th BNI)
Raised 1857 as the Extra Gurkha Regiment.
1891: 4th Gurkha Rifle Regiment (Two battalions from 1886). 1901: 4th Gurkha Rifles.
Green; faced black.
ALI MASJID, KABUL 1879, KANDAHAR 1880, AFGHANISTAN 1878–80, CHITRAL, PUNJAB FRONTIER, TIRAH, CHINA 1900.
(4th Gurkha Rifles)

16th BNI (20th)
Raised 1857 as Regiment of Lucknow from loyal elements of 13th, 48th and 71st BNI.
1864: 16th (The Lucknow Regiment) BNI. 1897: 16th (The Lucknow) Rajput Regiment, Bengal Infantry. 1901: 16th (Lucknow) Rajput Infantry. 1903: 16th Rajputs (The Lucknow Regiment).

Red; faced white.
Lucknow (with a turreted gateway), AFGHANISTAN 1878–80, BURMA 1885–87.
(10/7th Rajput Regiment)

17th BNI (21st)
Raised 1858 as the Loyal Purbeah Regiment from loyal elements of 3rd, 36th and 61st BNI.
1864: 17th (Loyal Purbeah) Regiment BNI. 1898: 17th (The Loyal) Regiment, Bengal Infantry. 1902: 17th Musulman Rajput Infantry (The Loyal Regiment). 1903: 17th The Loyal Regiment.
Red; faced white.
AFGHANISTAN 1879–80, SUAKIN 1885, TOFREK.
(Disbanded 1922)

18th BNI (22nd)
Raised 1795 as Calcutta Native Militia. At Mutiny, the Alipore Regiment.
1864: 18th (Alipore Regiment) BNI. 1885: 18th BNI. 1902: 18th Musulman Rajput Infantry. 1903: 18th Infantry.
Red; faced black.
BURMA 1885–87.
(4/9th Jat Regt.)

19th BNI (23rd)
Raised 1857 from companies of 2nd and 7th Punjab Police Battalions.
1864: 19th (Punjab) Regiment BNI. 1901: 19th Punjab Infantry. 1903: 19th Punjabis.
Red; faced dark blue.
AHMED KHEL, AFGHANISTAN 1878–80.
(1/14th Punjab Regt.)

20th BNI (24th)
Raised 1857 as 8th Punjab Infantry from 4th and 5th Punjab Infantry.
1864: 20th (Punjab) Regiment BNI. 1883: 20th (Duke of Cambridge's Own) (Punjab) Regiment BNI. 1901: 20th (Duke of Cambridge's Own) Punjab Infantry. 1904: 20th (Duke of Cambridge's Own) Brownlow's Punjabis.
Drab; faced green, 1905 emerald green.
TAKU FORTS, PEKIN, ALI MASJID, AFGHANISTAN 1878–80, EGYPT 1882, TEL-EL-KEBIR, PUNJAB FRONTIER, CHINA 1900.
(2/14th Punjab Regt.)

21st BNI (25th)
Raised 1857 as 9th Punjab Infantry from 3rd and 6th Punjab Infantry.

1864: 21st (Punjab) Regiment BNI. 1901: 21st Punjab Infantry. 1903: 21st Punjabis.
Drab; faced red, 1905 scarlet.
ABYSSINIA, AFGHANISTAN 1878–80.
(10/14th Punjab Regt.)

22nd BNI (26th)
Raised 1857 as 11th Punjab Infantry from 1st Sikh Infantry and 3rd Punjab Police Battalion.
1864: 22nd (Punjab) Regiment BNI. 1901: 22nd Punjab Infantry. 1903: 22nd Punjabis.
Red; faced buff, 1886 blue.
CHINA 1860–62, AFGHANISTAN 1879–80, PUNJAB FRONTIER.
(3/14th Punjab Regt.)

23rd BNI (27th)
Raised 1857 as 15th (Pioneer) Regiment of Punjab Infantry.
1864: 23rd (Punjab) Regiment BNI (Pioneers). 1901: 23rd Punjab Pioneers. 1903: 23rd Sikh Pioneers.
Drab; faced chocolate.
TAKU FORTS, PEKIN, ABYSSINIA, PEIWAR KOTAL, CHARASIAH, KABUL 1879, KANDAHAR 1880, AFGHANISTAN 1878–80, CHITRAL.
(1/3rd Sikh Pioneers)

24th BNI (28th)
Raised 1857 as 16th Punjab Infantry.
1864: 24th (Punjab) Regiment BNI. 1901: 24th Punjab Infantry. 1903: 24th Punjabis.
Red; faced white.
KANDAHAR 1880, AFGHANISTAN 1878–80, PUNJAB FRONTIER, MALAKAND, PEKIN 1900.
(4/14th Punjab Regt.)

25th BNI (29th)
Raised 1857 as Lahore Punjab Battalion and numbered 17th Punjab Infantry.
1864: 25th (Punjab) Regiment BNI. 1901: 25th Punjab Infantry. 1903: 25th Punjabis.
Red; faced white.
AHMED KHEL, KANDAHAR 1880, AFGHANISTAN 1878–80, CHITRAL.
(1/15th Punjab Regt.)

26th BNI (30th)
Raised 1857 as 18th Punjab Infantry.
1864: 26th (Punjab) Regiment BNI. 1901: 26th Punjab Infantry. 1903: 26th Punjabis.

Drab; faced red, 1905 scarlet.
AFGHANISTAN 1878–79, BURMA 1885–87.
(2/15th Punjab Regt.)

27th BNI (31st)
Raised 1857 as Regiment of Rawal Pindi and numbered 19th Punjab Infantry.
1864: 27th (Punjab) Regiment BNI. 1901: 27th Punjab Infantry. 1903: 27th Punjabis.
Drab; faced red, 1905 scarlet.
CHINA 1860–62, ALI MASJID, AFGHANISTAN 1878–80, BURMA 1885–87.
(3/15th Punjab Regt.)

28th BNI (32nd)
Raised 1857 as Ferozepore Punjab Battalion and numbered 20th Punjab Infantry.
1864: 28th (Punjab) Regiment BNI. 1901: 28th Punjab Infantry. 1903: 28th Punjabis.
Red; faced dark green, 1886 emerald green.
CHARASIAH, KABUL 1879, AFGHANISTAN 1878–80.
(4/15th Punjab Regt.)

29th BNI (33rd)
Raised 1857 as 21st Punjab Infantry.
1864: 29th (Punjab) Regiment BNI. 1901: 29th Punjab Infantry. 1903: 29th Punjabis.
Red; faced light blue, 1886 blue.
PEIWAR KOTAL, AFGHANISTAN 1878–80, CHITRAL.
(10/15th Punjab Regt.)

30th BNI (34th)
Raised 1857 as 22nd Punjab Infantry.
1864: 30th (Punjab) Regiment BNI. 1901: 30th Punjab Infantry. 1903: 30th Punjabis.
Red; faced buff, 1886 white.
AFGHANISTAN 1878–80, CHITRAL, PUNJAB FRONTIER, TIRAH.
(1/16th Punjab Regt.)

31st BNI (35th)
Raised 1857 as Cortlandt's Levy and numbered 23rd Punjab Infantry.
1864: 31st (Punjab) Regiment BNI. 1901: 31st Punjab Infantry.
1903: 31st Punjabis.
Red; faced dark green, 1886 white.
AFGHANISTAN 1879–80, PUNJAB FRONTIER, MALAKAND.
(2/16th Punjab Regt.)

20

32nd BNI (36th)
Raised 1857 as Punjab Sappers, numbered 24th (Pioneer) Punjab Infantry in 1858.
1864: 32nd (Punjab) Regiment BNI (Pioneers).
1901: 32nd Punjab Pioneers. 1903: 32nd Sikh Pioneers.
Red; faced dark blue.
Delhi, Lucknow, AFGHANISTAN 1878–80, CHITRAL.
(2/3rd Sikh Pioneers)

33rd BNI (37th)
Raised 1857 as the Allahabad Levy.
1864: 33rd (Allahabad) Regiment BNI. 1885: 33rd Bengal Infantry. 1890: 33rd (Punjabi Mahomedan) Regiment, Bengal Infantry. 1901: 33rd Punjab Infantry. 1903: 33rd Punjabis.
Red; faced white. 1905 Drab; faced green, 1911 emerald green.
BURMA 1885.
(3/16th Punjab Regt.)

34th BNI (38th)
Raised 1858 as the Fategarh Levy.
1864: 34th (Fategarh) Regiment BNI. 1882: Disbanded.
Red; faced dark blue.

35th BNI (39th)
Raised 1858 as the Mynpoorie Levy.

British and Indian officers, NCOs and men, 20th Punjab Infantry, 1890, in full dress drab tunics, faced green. Drab turbans with green fringe. (National Army Museum)

1864: 35th (Mynpoorie) Regiment BNI. 1882: Disbanded.
Red; faced white.

36th BNI (40th)
Raised 1858 as the Bareilly Levy.
1864: 36th (Bareilly) Regiment BNI. 1882: Disbanded.
Red; faced blue.

37th BNI (41st)
Raised 1858 as the Meerut Levy.
1864: 37th (Meerut) Regiment BNI. 1882: Disbanded.
Red; faced white.

38th BNI (42nd)
Raised 1858 as the Agra Levy.
1864: 38th (Agra) Regiment BNI. 1890: 38th (Dogra) Regiment, Bengal Infantry. 1901: 38th Dogra Infantry. 1903: 38th Dogras.
Red; faced dark blue, 1892 yellow.
PUNJAB FRONTIER, MALAKAND.
(2/17th Dogra Regt.)

39th BNI (43rd)
Raised 1858 as the Aligarh Levy.

The Band of the 3rd Infantry, Hyderabad Contingent, in khaki, c. 1890. These men make an interesting contrast with those of the 'martial races'. (Collection R. G. Harris)

1864: 39th (The Aligarh) Regiment BNI. 1890: Disbanded.
Red; faced dark blue.
AFGHANISTAN 1878–80.

40th BNI (44th)
Raised 1858 as the Shahjehanpur Levy.
1864: 40th (Shahjehanpur) Regiment BNI. 1890: 40th (Baluch) Regiment, Bengal Infantry. 1892: 40th (Pathan) Regiment, Bengal Infantry. 1901: 40th Punjab Infantry. 1903: 40th Pathans.
Red; faced white. 1892 Drab; faced green, 1911 emerald green.
(5/14th Punjab Regt.)

41st BNI (45th)
Raised 1858 as 1st Gwalior Regiment.
1864: 41st (Gwalior) Regiment BNI. 1882: Disbanded.
Red; faced cavalry grey.

42nd BNI (46th)
Raised 1817 as the Cuttack Legion. At Mutiny, 1st Assam Light Infantry.
1885: 42nd (Assam) Regiment, Bengal Light Infantry. 1886: 42nd (Gurkha) Light Infantry. 1891: 42nd Gurkha (Rifle) Regiment, Bengal Infantry. 1901: 42nd Gurkha Rifles. 1903: 6th Gurkha Rifles. (Two battalions 1904.)

Green; faced black.
BURMA 1885–87.
(6th Gurkha Rifles)

Deoli Irregular Force (Infantry)
Raised 1857.
1903: 42nd Deoli Regiment.
Green; faced red.
(Disbanded 1922)

43rd BNI (47th)
Raised 1835 as the Assam Sebundy Corps. At Mutiny, 2nd Assam Light Infantry.
1864: 43rd (Assam) Regiment BN Light Infantry. 1886: 43rd Gurkha Light Infantry, Bengal Infantry. 1891: 43rd Gurkha (Rifle) Regiment, Bengal Infantry. 1901: 43rd Gurkha Rifles. 1903: 7th Gurkha Rifles. 1907: 2/8th Gurkha Rifles.
Green; faced black.
(2/8th Gurkha Rifles)

Erinpura Irregular Force (Infantry)
Raised 1860.
1903: 43rd Erinpura Regiment.
Green; faced red. Red trousers.
(Disbanded 1922)

44th BNI (48th)
Raised 1824 as the Sylhet Local Battalion. At Mutiny, 11th Sylhet Local Light Infantry.
1864: 44th Sylhet BN Light Infantry. 1886: 44th Gurkha Light Infantry. 1891: 44th Gurkha (Rifle) Regiment, Bengal Infantry. 1901: 44th Gurkha

Rifles. 1903: 8th Gurkha Rifles.
Green; faced black.
BURMA 1885–87.
(8th Gurkha Rifles)

Ajmer and Mharwara Police Corps
Raised 1822 as 14th Mharwara Local Battalion. At Mutiny, the Mharwara Battalion.
1871: The Mharwara Battalion. 1903: 44th Mharwara Regiment.
Red; faced green, 1870 French grey, 1891 yellow.
Central India, AFGHANISTAN 1878–80.
(Disbanded 1922)

Bengal Military Police Battalion
Raised 1856 and numbered 1st Bengal Military Police Battalion in 1858.

The Queen's Own Corps of Guides (Infantry), Frontier Force, 1897. Sepoy in khaki and poshteen; subadar in full dress, drab tunic faced red; lance-naik and havildar in musketry order. (National Army Museum)
Left:
32nd (Punjab) Bengal Infantry (Pioneers), 1897. Subadar in full dress of red turban and tunic faced blue, blue trousers and puttees; havildar and sepoys in khaki marching order with pioneer tools and equipment. (National Army Museum)

1864: 45th (Rattray's Sikh) Regiment, BNI. 1901: 45th Rattray's Sikh Infantry. 1903: 45th Rattray's Sikhs.
1859 Drab; faced blue. 1870 Red; faced light buff, 1886 white.
Defence of Arrah, ALI MASJID, AFGHANISTAN 1879–80, PUNJAB FRONTIER, MALAKAND.
(3/11th Sikh Regt.)

In 1887 the following five regiments were raised and took the numbers of the 34th-37th BNI which had been disbanded in 1882 (see above) and the 39th BNI, disbanded in 1890.

34th (Punjab) Regiment, Bengal Infantry Pioneers
1901: 34th Punjab Pioneers. 1903: 34th Sikh Pioneers.
Red; faced dark blue.
CHITRAL, PUNJAB FRONTIER, CHINA 1900.
(3/3rd Sikh Pioneers)

35th (Sikh) Regiment, Bengal Infantry
1901: 35th Sikh Infantry. 1903: 35th Sikhs.
Red; faced yellow.
PUNJAB FRONTIER, MALAKAND.
(10/11th Sikh Regt.)

36th (Sikh) Regiment, Bengal Infantry
1901: 36th Sikh Infantry. 1903: 36th Sikhs.
Scarlet; faced yellow.
PUNJAB FRONTIER, SAMANA, TIRAH.
(4/11th Sikh Regt.)

37th (Dogra) Regiment, Bengal Infantry
1901: 37th Dogra Infantry. 1903: 37th Dogras.
Scarlet; faced yellow.
CHITRAL, PUNJAB FRONTIER.
(1/17th Dogra Regt.)

2nd Battalion 3rd Gurkha Rifles
1890: 39th (The Garhwali) Regiment, Bengal Infantry. 1901: 39th Garhwal Rifles. (Two battalions 1901.)
Green; faced black.
PUNJAB FRONTIER.
(1/18th Royal Garhwal Rifles)

In 1900–02 the following five regiments were raised, the senior taking the number of the 41st BNI, previously disbanded in 1882.

41st (Dogra) Regiment, Bengal Infantry (1900)
1901: 41st Dogra Infantry. 1903: 41st Dogras.
Scarlet; faced yellow.
(3/17th Dogra Regt.)

46th (Punjab) Regiment, Bengal Infantry (1900)
1901: 46th Punjab Infantry. 1903: 46th Punjabis.
Drab; faced green, 1911 emerald green.
(10/16th Punjab Regt.)

47th Sikh Infantry (1901)
1903: 47th Sikhs.
Scarlet; faced yellow.
(5/11th Sikh Regt.)

48th Bengal Pioneers (1901)
1903: 48th Pioneers.
Scarlet; faced emerald green, 1903 black.
(4th Bn. Bombay Pioneers)

8th Gurkha Rifles (1902)
1903: 2nd Battalion 10th Gurkha Rifles. 1907: 7th
Gurkha Rifles. (Two battalions.)
Green; faced black.
(7th Gurkha Rifles)

PUNJAB FRONTIER FORCE (PFF)

Punjab Irregular Force (PIF) up to 1865, Punjab
Frontier Force thereafter. From 1903, Frontier
Force (FF) only. First titles as in 1865.

Corps of Guides PFF (Infantry)
Raised 1846 as Corps of Guides. At Mutiny, Corps
of Guides PIF.
1876: The Queen's Own Corps of Guides PFF.
1904: The Queen's Own Corps of Guides
(Lumsden's). 1911: Queen Victoria's Own Corps
of Guides (FF) (Lumsden's) Infantry.
Drab; faced, 1859 drab, 1870 piped red, 1882 faced
red, 1905 red velvet (officers) red cloth (soldiers),
1908 scarlet.
Punjab, Mooltan, Goojerat, Delhi, ALI MASJID,
KABUL 1879, AFGHANISTAN 1878–80, CHITRAL,
PUNJAB FRONTIER, MALAKAND.
(5th (QVO Corps of Guides)/12th Frontier Force
Regt.)

1st Sikh Infantry PFF
Raised 1846 as 1st Infantry, Frontier Brigade. At
Mutiny, 1st Sikh Infantry PIF.
1901: 1st Sikh Infantry. 1903: 51st Sikhs (FF).

Drab; faced yellow.
Punjab, ALI MASJID, AFGHANISTAN 1878–79, PEKIN
1900.
(1/12th Frontier Force Regt.)

2nd or Hill Regiment Sikh Infantry PFF
Raised 1846 as 2nd Infantry, Frontier Brigade. At
Mutiny, 2nd or Hill Regiment of Sikh Infantry
PIF.
1901: 2nd or Hill Sikh Infantry. 1903: 52nd Sikhs
(FF).
Drab; faced black, 1870 piped red, 1882 faced red,
1905 scarlet.
Punjab, AHMED KHEL, KANDAHAR 1880, AFGHANIS-
TAN 1879–80.
(2/12th Frontier Force Regt.)

3rd Sikh Infantry PFF
Raised 1846–47 as 3rd Infantry, Frontier Brigade.
At Mutiny, 3rd Sikh Infantry PIF.
1901: 3rd Sikh Infantry. 1903: 53rd Sikhs (FF).
Drab; faced yellow, 1870 black.
KABUL 1879, KANDAHAR 1880, AFGHANISTAN
1879–80, PUNJAB FRONTIER, TIRAH.
(3/12th Frontier Force Regt.)

4th Sikh Infantry PFF
Raised 1846–47 as 4th Infantry, Frontier Brigade.
At Mutiny, 4th Sikh Infantry PIF.
1901: 4th Sikh Infantry. 1903: 54th Sikhs (FF).
Drab; faced dark green, 1888 emerald green.
Pegu, Delhi, CHITRAL.
(4/12th Frontier Force Regt.)

1st Infantry PFF
Raised 1849 as 1st Punjab Infantry. At Mutiny, 1st
Infantry PIF.
1903: 55th Coke's Rifles (FF).
Green; faced green, 1870 piped red, 1905 piped
scarlet.
Delhi, AFGHANISTAN 1878–79.
(1/13th Frontier Force Rifles)

2nd Infantry PFF
Raised 1849 as 2nd Punjab Infantry. At Mutiny,
2nd Infantry PIF.
1901: 2nd Punjab Infantry. 1903: 56th Infantry
(FF). 1906: 56th Punjab Rifles (FF).
Drab; faced black.
Delhi, Lucknow, PEIWAR KOTAL, AFGHANISTAN

1 Havildar, 21st Madras Native Infantry, 1861
2 British Captain, 10th Bengal Native Infantry, c.1865
3 Sepoy, 1st Infantry, Punjab Irregular Force, c.1865

1

2

3

JEFFREY BURN

A

1 Sepoy, 15th Punjab Infantry, 1860
2 Sepoy, 27th Bombay Native Infantry (1st Baluch Regiment), 1868
3 Sepoy, 3rd Sikh Infantry, Punjab Irregular Force, 1863

B

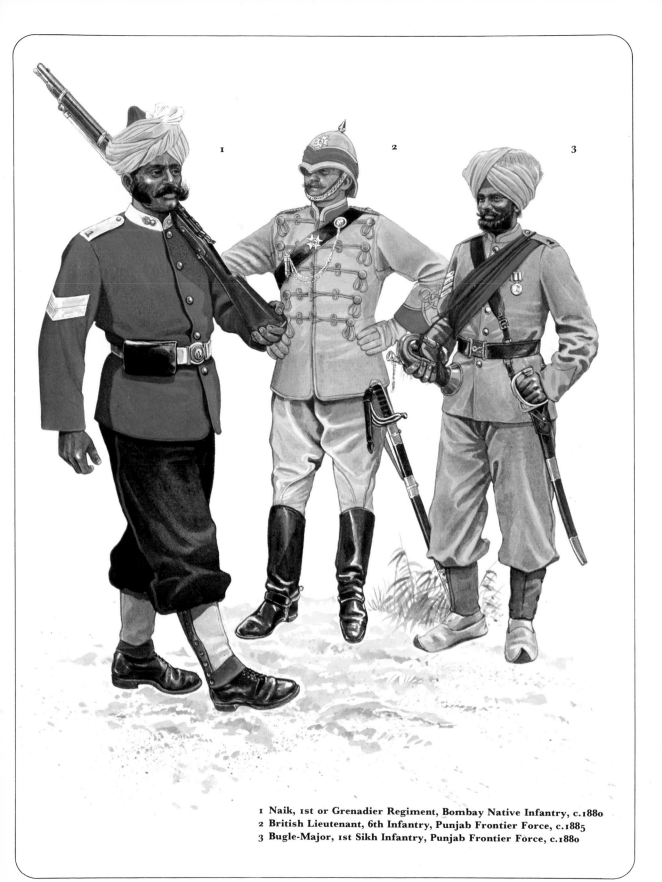

1 Naik, 1st or Grenadier Regiment, Bombay Native Infantry, c.1880
2 British Lieutenant, 6th Infantry, Punjab Frontier Force, c.1885
3 Bugle-Major, 1st Sikh Infantry, Punjab Frontier Force, c.1880

1 Sepoy, 45th (Rattray's Sikh) Regiment, Bengal Native Infantry, 1879
2 British Officer, 5th Infantry, Punjab Frontier Force, 1880
3 Sepoy, 23rd (Punjab) Regiment, Bengal Native Infantry (Pioneers), 1880

D

1 **Sepoy, 26th Punjab Regiment, Bengal Infantry, 1896**
2 **Havildar, 15th Bengal Infantry (Ludhiana Sikhs), 1898**
3 **British Major, 29th (Duke of Connaught's Own) Bombay Infantry**
   (2nd Baluch Regiment), 1896

E

1 Sepoy, 1st Madras Pioneers, 1886
2 Sepoy, 36th (Sikh) Regiment, Bengal Infantry, 1897
3 Havildar, The Queen's Own Corps of Guides (Infantry),
  Punjab Frontier Force, 1897

1 Havildar, 125th Napier's Rifles, c.1905
2 Subadar, 16th Rajputs (The Lucknow Regiment), c.1905
3 Naik, 57th Wilde's Rifles (Frontier Force), 1914

JEFFREY BURN

G

1 Jemadar, 14th Bengal Infantry (Ferozepore Sikhs), 1900
2 Sepoy, 41st Dogras, c.1910
3 Lance-Naik, 39th Garhwal Rifles, 1914

H

1878–79, PUNJAB FRONTIER, TIRAH.
(2/13th Frontier Force Rifles)

3rd Infantry PFF
Raised 1849 as 3rd Punjab Infantry. At Mutiny, 3rd Infantry PIF.
1882: Disbanded.
Drab; faced drab, piped green.

4th Infantry PFF
Raised 1849 as 4th Punjab Infantry. At Mutiny, 4th Infantry PIF.
1901: 4th Punjab Infantry. 1903: 57th Wilde's Rifles (FF).
Drab; faced French grey, 1870 Prussian blue.
Delhi, Lucknow, AFGHANISTAN 1879–80, CHINA 1900.
(4/13th Frontier Force Rifles)

5th Infantry PFF
Raised 1849 as 5th Punjab Infantry. At Mutiny, 5th Infantry PIF.
1901: 5th Punjab Infantry. 1903: 58th Vaughan's Rifles (FF).
Drab; faced green, 1905 emerald green.
PEIWAR KOTAL, CHARASIAH, KABUL 1879, AFGHANIS-TAN 1878–80.
(5/13th Frontier Force Rifles)

6th Infantry PFF
Raised 1843 as the Scinde Camel Corps. At Mutiny, 6th Punjab Infantry.
1901: 6th Punjab Infantry. 1903: 59th Scinde Rifles (FF).
Red; faced rifle-green. 1870 Drab; faced red, 1898 scarlet.
(6/13th Frontier Force Rifles)

5th Gurkha Regiment or Hazara Gurkha Battalion PIF (1861, October)
Raised 1858 as 25th Punjab Infantry or Hazara Gurkha Battalion. In May 1861, 7th Infantry, Hazara Gurkha Battalion PIF.
1887: 5th Gurkha Regiment PFF. (Two battalions 1886.) 1891: 5th Gurkha (Rifle) Regiment PFF.
1901: 5th Gurkha Rifles. 1903: 5th Gurkha Rifles (FF).
Green; faced black.
PEIWAR KOTAL, CHARASIAH, KABUL 1879, KAN-DAHAR 1880, AFGHANISTAN 1878–80, PUNJAB FRON-TIER.

(5th Royal Gurkha Rifles FF)

MADRAS ARMY

The titles under which regiments appear are those in use in 1861, which were the same as those acquired in 1824, since there were no changes after the Mutiny.

1st Regiment of Madras Native Infantry (MNI)
Raised 1758 as 1st Bn. Coast Sepoys.
1883: 1st MNI (Pioneers). 1901: 1st Pioneers.
1903: 61st Pioneers. 1906: 61st Prince of Wales's Own Pioneers. 1910: 61st King George's Own Pioneers.
Red; faced white.
Carnatic, Mysore, Seringapatam, Seetabuldee, Nagpore, Ava, Pegu, Central India, AFGHANISTAN 1878–80, BURMA 1885–87, CHINA 1900.
(1st Bn. Corps of Madras Pioneers)

2nd MNI
Raised 1759 as 3rd Bn. Coast Sepoys.
1903: 62nd Punjabis.
Red; faced deep green, 1882 green, 1898 emerald green.
Carnatic, Mysore, Assaye, Nagpore, China.
(1/1st Punjab Regt.)

3rd Palamcottah Light Infantry Regiment MNI
Raised 1759 as 4th Bn. Coast Sepoys.
1885: 3rd or Palamcottah Regiment, MN Light Infantry. 1903: 63rd Palamcottah Light Infantry.
Red; faced dark green, 1882 green, 1898 emerald green.
Carnatic, Sholinghur, Mysore, Mahidpoor, Ava, BURMA 1885–87, CHINA 1900.
(Disbanded 1922)

4th MNI
Raised 1759 as 5th Bn. Coast Sepoys.
1883: 4th MNI (Pioneers). 1901: 4th Madras Pioneers. 1903: 64th Pioneers.
Red; faced orange, 1882 yellow, 1895 white.
Carnatic, Sholinghur, Mysore, Assaye, AFGHANIS-TAN 1879–80.
(2nd Bn. Corps of Madras Pioneers)

5th MNI
Raised 1759 as 6th Bn. Coast Sepoys.
1903: 65th Carnatic Infantry. 1904: Disbanded.
Red; faced black, 1882 yellow.

Carnatic, Sholinghur, Mysore, Pegu, BURMA 1885–87.

6th MNI
Raised 1761 as 7th Bn. Coast Sepoys.
1903: 66th Punjabis.
Red; faced buff, 1882 white, 1905 green, 1914 emerald green.
Carnatic, Sholinghur, Mysore, Seringapatam, Bourbon, China.
(2/1st Punjab Regt.)

7th MNI
Raised 1761 as 8th Bn. Coast Sepoys.
1903: 67th Punjabis.
Red; faced, 1857 sky-blue, 1882 yellow, 1905 green, 1914 emerald green.
Carnatic, Mysore, Ava.
(1/2nd Punjab Regt.)

8th MNI
Raised 1761 as 9th Bn. Coast Sepoys.
1901: 8th Madras Infantry. 1902: 8th Gurkhas. 1902: Disbanded.
Red; faced bright yellow, 1882 white. 1902 Green; faced black.
Carnatic, Sholinghur, Seringapatam, Assaye.

9th MNI
Raised 1762–65 as 10th Bn. Coast Sepoys.
1903: 69th Punjabis.
Red; faced gosling-green, 1882 dark green, 1891 emerald green.
Carnatic, Sholinghur, Mysore, Ava, Pegu.
(2/2nd Punjab Regt.)

10th MNI
Raised 1766 as 14th Bn. Coast Sepoys.
1891: Disbanded.
Red; faced red, 1882 yellow.
Ambour, Assaye, Ava.

11th MNI
Raised 1767 as 15th Bn. Coast Sepoys.
1902: 11th Coorg Infantry. 1903: 71st Coorg Rifles. 1904: Disbanded.
Red; faced, 1853 dark green, 1882 green, 1891 emerald green. 1903 Green; faced scarlet.
Seringapatam.

12th MNI
Raised 1767 as 16th Bn. Coast Sepoys.

1890: 2nd Burma Battalion. 1891: 12th Regiment (2nd Burma Battalion) Madras Infantry. 1901: 12th Burma Infantry. 1903: 72nd Punjabis.
Red; faced pale buff, 1882 white. 1892 Drab; faced white.
Carnatic, Sholinghur, Ava, BURMA 1885–87.
(3/2nd Punjab Regt.)

13th MNI
Raised 1776 as 13th Carnatic Battalion.
1903: 73rd Carnatic Infantry.
Red; faced white.
Carnatic, Sholinghur, Mysore, Seringapatam, BURMA 1885–87.
(1/3rd Madras Regt.)

14th MNI
Raised 1776 as 14th Carnatic Battalion.
1903: 74th Punjabis.
Red; faced buff, 1882 white, 1905 green, 1911 emerald green.
Carnatic, Sholinghur, Mysore, Mahidpoor, China, BURMA 1885–87.

15th MNI
Raised 1776 as 15th Carnatic Battalion.
1903: 75th Carnatic Infantry.
Red; faced orange, 1882 yellow.
Carnatic, Sholinghur, Mysore, AFGHANISTAN 1879–80, BURMA 1885–87.
(2/3rd Madras Regt.)

16th MNI
Raised 1776 as 16th Carnatic Battalion.
1903: 76th Punjabis.
Red; faced black, 1882 yellow, 1905 green, 1911 emerald green.
Carnatic, Sholinghur, Mysore, Seringapatam, Ava, BURMA 1885–87.
(3/1st Punjab Regt.)

17th MNI
Raised 1777 as 17th Carnatic Battalion.
1902: 1st Moplah Rifles. 1903: 77th Moplah Rifles. 1907: Disbanded.
Red; faced white. 1903 Green; faced scarlet.
Carnatic, Sholinghur, Nagpore, BURMA 1885–87.

18th MNI
Raised 1777 as 19th Carnatic Battalion.
1864: Disbanded.
Red; faced red.   Ava.

19th MNI

Raised 1777 as 20th Carnatic Battalion.

1903: 79th Carnatic Infantry.

Red; faced sky-blue, 1882 yellow.

Carnatic, Sholinghur, Mysore, Seringapatam.
Pegu, Central India.

(3/3rd Madras Regt.)

20th MNI

Raised 1777 as 21st Carnatic Battalion.

1903: 80th Carnatic Infantry.

Red; faced deep green, 1882 green, 1898 emerald green.

Carnatic, Sholinghur, Mysore, Seringapatam.

(Disbanded 1922)

21st MNI

Raised 1786 as 28th Madras Battalion.

1891: 21st Madras Infantry (Pioneers). 1903: 81st Pioneers.

Red; faced pale buff, 1882 white.

Mysore, Seringapatam, Nagpore, AFGHANISTAN 1878–80, BURMA 1885–87, PUNJAB FRONTIER, TIRAH.

(10th Bn. Corps of Madras Pioneers)

22nd MNI

Raised 1788 as 29th Madras Battalion.

1903: 82nd Punjabis.

Red; faced buff, 1905 green, 1911 emerald green.

29th Bombay Infantry (2nd Baluch), 1897. Naik (Punjabi Mussulman) in review order of green turban and tunic, red trousers; sepoy (Afridi) in marching order; bugler (Khattack) in drill order; sepoy (Baluchi), drill order; jemadar (Brahui), review order. The long hair of the Baluchi was tied up under the turban on parade. (*Navy & Army Illustrated*/Collection R. G. Harris)

2nd Punjab Infantry, Frontier Force, in action during the Tirah campaign 1897. Watercolour by C. J. Staniland. (National Army Museum)

Mysore, Seringapatam, Ava.
(5/1st Punjab Regt.)

23rd Wallajahbad Light Infantry MNI

Raised 1794 as 33rd Madras Battalion.

1903: 83rd Wallajahbad Light Infantry.

Red; faced deep green, 1882 green, 1898 emerald green.

Seringapatam, Nagpore, BURMA 1885–87.

(4/3rd Madras Regt.)

Jemadar, 4th (Rifle Regiment) Bombay Infantry in full dress, c. 1890. Rifle-green uniform faced red, black pouch belt. Green turban with red kulla. Watercolour by A. C. Lovett. (National Army Museum)

24th MNI
Raised 1794 as 34th Madras Battalion.
1903: 84th Punjabis.
Red; faced willow green, 1870 dark green, 1882 green, 1898 emerald green.
Seringapatam, Assaye, Bourbon.
(10/1st Punjab Regt.)

25th MNI
Raised 1794 as 35th Madras Battalion.
1902: 2nd Moplah Rifles. 1903: 78th Moplah Rifles.
1907: Disbanded.
Red; faced dark green, 1882 green, 1898 emerald green. 1904 Green; faced scarlet.
BURMA 1885–87.

26th MNI
Raised 1794 as 36th Madras Battalion.
1903: 86th Carnatic Infantry.
Red; faced dark green, 1882 green, 1898 emerald

green.
Nagpore, Kemendine, Ava, Pegu, BURMA 1885–87.
(10/3rd Madras Regt.)

27th MNI
Raised 1798 as 1st Extra Battalion.
1903: 87th Punjabis.
Red; faced black, 1882 yellow, 1905 green, 1911 emerald green.
Mahidpore, Lucknow, BURMA 1885–87.
(5/2nd Punjab Regt.)

28th MNI
Raised 1798 as 2nd Extra Battalion.
1903: 88th Carnatic Infantry.
Red; faced black, 1882 yellow.
Mahidpore, Nagpore, Ava, CHINA 1900.
(Disbanded 1922)

29th MNI
Raised 1798 as 3rd Extra Battalion.
1893: 29th Regiment (7th Burma Battalion) Madras Infantry. 1901: 29th Burma Infantry.
1903: 89th Punjabis.
Red; faced white. 1897 Drab; faced blue.
(1/8th Punjab Regt.)

30th MNI
Raised 1799 as the Masulipatam Battalion.
1892: 30th Regiment (5th Burma Battalion) Madras Infantry. 1903: 90th Punjabis.
Red; faced white. 1897 Drab; faced blue.
Ava, AFGHANISTAN 1878–80, BURMA 1885–87.
(2/8th Punjab Regt.)

31st Trichinopoly Madras Light Infantry
Raised 1800 as 1/16th MNI.
1892: 31st Regiment (6th Burma Battalion) Madras Light Infantry. 1901: 31st Burma Light Infantry. 1903: 91st Punjabis (Light Infantry).
Red; faced dark green, 1882 green. 1894 Drab; faced cherry.
Mahidpoor, CHINA 1900.
(3/8th Punjab Regt.)

32nd MNI
Raised 1800 as 2/16th MNI.
1890: 4th Regiment of Burma Infantry. 1891: 32nd Regiment (4th Burma Battalion) Madras Infantry.
1901: 32nd Burma Infantry. 1903: 92nd Punjabis.
Red; faced pale yellow, 1882 yellow. 1892 Blue; faced scarlet. 1897 Drab; faced white.   Ava.

(4/8th Punjab Regt.)

33rd MNI
Raised 1800 as 1/17th MNI.
1890: 3rd Regiment of Burma Infantry. 1891: 33rd
Regiment (3rd Burma Battalion) Madras Infantry.
1902: 33rd Burma Infantry. 1903: 93rd Burma
Infantry.
Red; faced black, 1882 yellow. 1897 Drab; faced
yellow.
(5/8th Punjab Regt.)

34th Chicacole Light Infantry MNI
Raised 1800 as 2/17th MNI.
1882: Disbanded.
Red; faced dark green.
Ava.

The following seven regiments, raised between
1800–03, were all disbanded in 1882. Only the
facing colours and battle honours are given. All
uniformed red.

35th MNI. Pale buff. Pegu.
36th MNI. Pale buff. Ava.
37th MNI. Blue. China.
38th MNI. Buff. Ava.
39th MNI. Dark green. Seetabuldee, Nagpore.
40th MNI. Dark green.
41st MNI. Deep green. China.

The following eleven regiments, raised between
1803–26, were all disbanded between 1862–64.
Shortened details as above.
42nd MNI. Bright yellow. (1864)
43rd MNI. Pale yellow. (1864)
44th MNI. Pale yellow. (1864)
45th MNI. White. (1862)
46th MNI. White. (1862)
47th MNI. Pale buff. (1862)
48th MNI. Pale buff. (1862)
49th MNI. Bright yellow. (1862)
50th MNI. Bright yellow. (1862)
51st MNI. White. (1862)
52nd MNI. Pale buff. (1862)

The following regiment was raised in 1890 from
the Kubo Valley Police Battalion:
1st Regiment of Burma Infantry
1891: 10th Regiment (1st Burma Battalion)
Madras Infantry. 1892: 10th Regiment (1st Burma

Indian officers of the 36th Sikh Infantry in full dress, 1901. The
centre panel of the tunic was square-cut in the skirt from the
late 1890s. Note the steel quoits in the turbans. (Collection R. G.
Harris)

Rifles) Madras Infantry. 1895: 10th Regiment (1st
Burma Gurkha Rifles) Madras Infantry. 1901:
10th Gurkha Rifles. (Two battalions, 1908.)
Green; faced black.
(10th Gurkha Rifles)

HYDERABAND CONTINGENT (HC)

First two regiments raised by Mr Russell, British
Resident in Hyderabad. From 1826, under the
Nizam of Hyderabad. Taken into the Indian Line
in 1903. First titles as in 1861.

1st Infantry HC
Raised 1813 as 1st Battalion, Russell's Brigade.
1903: 94th Russell's Infantry.
Red; faced dark green.
Mahidpoor, Nowah.
(1/19th Hyderabad Regt.)

2nd Infantry HC
Raised 1813 as 2nd Battalion, Russell's Brigade.
1903: 95th Russell's Infantry.
Red; faced dark green.
Mahidpoor, Nowah, BURMA 1885–87.
(10/19th Hyderabad Regt.)

3rd Infantry HC
Raised 1797 as 2nd Battalion, Aurangabad Division.
1903: 96th Berar Infantry.
Red; faced dark green.
Nowah, Central India, BURMA 1885–87.
(2/19th Hyderabad Regt.)

4th Infantry HC
Raised 1794 as 3rd Battalion, Aurangabad Division.
1903: 97th Deccan Infantry.
Red; faced dark green.
Nagpore.
(3/19th Hyderabad Regt.)

5th Infantry HC
Raised 1788 as Salabat Khan's Regiment.
1903: 98th Infantry.
Red; faced dark green.
Central India, CHINA 1900.
(4/19th Hyderabad Regt.)

6th Infantry HC
Raised 1788 as 2nd Battalion, Ellichpur Brigade.
1903: 99th Deccan Infantry.
Red; faced dark green.
(5/19th Hyderabad Regt.)

BOMBAY ARMY

The titles under which regiments appear are those in use in 1861, which in the case of regiments numbered 1st–25th were those acquired in 1824, since there were no changes after the Mutiny.

1st or Grenadier Regiment of Bombay Native Infantry (ByNI)
Raised 1778 from grenadier companies of other regiments and designated 8th Battalion Bombay Sepoys.
1903: 101st Grenadiers.
Red; faced white.
Mangalore, Mysore, Hyderabad, KANDAHAR 1880, AFGHANISTAN 1878–80, BURMA 1885–87.
(1/4th Bombay Grenadiers)

2nd or Grenadier Regiment ByNI
Raised 1796 as 13th Bn. ByNI.
1876: 2nd (Prince of Wales's Own) ByNI (Grenadiers). 1903: 102nd Prince of Wales's Own Grenadiers. 1906: 102nd King Edward's Own Grenadiers.
Red; faced white.
Egypt, Kirkee, Corygaum, ABYSSINIA.
(2/4th Bombay Grenadiers)

3rd ByNI
Raised 1768 as 2nd Bn. Bombay Sepoys.
1871: 3rd ByN Light Infantry. 1903: 103rd

Mahratta Light Infantry.
Red; faced sky-blue, 1888 blue, 1895 black.
Mysore, Seedaseer, Seringapatam, Beni Boo Ali, Punjab, Mooltan, Goojerat, ABYSSINIA.
(1/5th Mahratta Light Infantry)

4th ByNI or Rifle Corps
Raised 1775 as 5th Bn. Bombay Sepoys.
1889: 4th Regiment (1st Battalion Rifle Regiment) of Bombay Infantry. 1901: 4th Bombay Rifles. 1903: 104th Wellesley's Rifles.
Green; faced red.
Mysore, Seringapatam, Bourbon, Beni Boo Ali, Punjab, Mooltan, Persia, Reshire, Bushire, Kooshab, Central India, KANDAHAR 1880, AFGHANISTAN 1878–80, BRITISH EAST AFRICA 1898.
(1/6th Rajputana Rifles)

5th ByN Light Infantry
Raised 1788 as 3rd Bn. Bombay Sepoys.
1903: 105th Mahratta Light Infantry.
Red; faced black.
Mysore, Seedaseer, Seringapatam, Beni Boo Ali, Kahun, CHINA 1860–62, AFGHANISTAN 1879–80, BURMA 1885–87.
(2/5th Mahratta Light Infantry)

6th ByNI
Raised 1775 as 6th Bn. Bombay Sepoys.
1882: Disbanded.
Red; faced black.
Seringapatam.

7th ByNI
Raised 1788 as 4th Bn. Bombay Sepoys.
1900: 7th Bombay Infantry (Pioneers). 1903: 107th Pioneers.
Red; faced white.
Mysore, Seedaseer, Seringapatam, Beni Boo Ali, BURMA 1885–87.
(1/2nd Bombay Pioneers)

8th ByNI
Raised 1768 as 1st Bn. Bombay Sepoys.
1903: 108th Infantry.
Red; faced white.
Mysore, Hyderabad, AFGHANISTAN 1879–80.
(3/4th Bombay Grenadiers)

9th ByNI
Raised 1788 as 5th Bn. Bombay Sepoys.

1903: 109th Infantry.
Red; faced black.
Mysore, Seringapatam, Punjab, Mooltan, AFGHANISTAN 1879–80.
(4/4th Bombay Grenadiers)

10th ByNI
Raised 1797 as 2/5th ByNI.
1871: 10th Bombay (Light) Infantry. 1903: 110th Mahratta Light Infantry.
Red; faced black.
Central India, ABYSSINIA, AFGHANISTAN 1879–80.
(3/5th Mahratta Light Infantry)

11th ByNI
Raised 1796 as 1/6th ByNI.
1882: Disbanded.
Red; faced pale buff.
Persia.

12th ByNI
Raised 1798 as 2/6th ByNI.
1903: 112th Infantry.
Red; faced deep buff, 1884 yellow.
Kirkee, Meanee, Hyderabad, Central India.
(5/4th Bombay Grenadiers)

13th ByNI
Raised 1800 as 1/7th ByNI.

Left:
Part of the Indian Contingent for the Coronation of King Edward VII, 1902. Jemadar and men of the 3rd Bombay Light Infantry and men of the 39th Garhwal Rifles. The latter's uniform resembled that of the Gurkha Rifles. (Collection R. G. Harris)

Right:
Officer of the 15th (Ludhiana) Sikh Infantry in khaki on arrival at Southampton for the 1902 Coronation. (National Army Museum)

1903: 113th Infantry.
Red; faced buff, 1882 yellow.
Egypt, Kirkee, Beni Boo Ali, Central India, AFGHANISTAN 1878–80.
(10/4th Bombay Grenadiers)

14th ByNI
Raised 1800 as 2/7th ByNI.
1903: 114th Mahrattas.
Red; faced light buff, 1882 yellow.
(10/5th Mahratta Light Infantry)

15th ByNI
Raised 1800 as 1/8th ByNI.
1882: Disbanded.
Red; faced light buff.
Persia.

16th ByNI
Raised 1800 as 2/8th ByNI.
1903: 116th Mahrattas.

Red; faced light buff, 1882 yellow.
AFGHANISTAN 1879–80, BRITISH EAST AFRICA 1901.
(4/5th Mahratta Light Infantry)

17th ByNI
Raised 1803 as 1/9th ByNI.
1903; 117th Mahrattas.
Red; faced pale yellow, 1882 yellow.
(5/5th Mahratta Light Infantry)

18th ByNI
Raised 1803 as 2/9th ByNI.
1882: Disbanded.
Red; faced yellow, 1871 pale yellow.
Beni Boo Ali, ABYSSINIA.

19th ByNI
Raised 1817 as 1/10 ByNI.
1903: 119th Infantry (The Mooltan Regiment).
Red; faced deep yellow, 1882 yellow.
Ghuznee, Afghanistan, Punjab, Mooltan, Goojerat, KANDAHAR 1880, AFGHANISTAN 1878–80.
(2/9th Jat Regt.)

20th ByNI
Raised 1817 as 2/10th ByNI.
1903: 120th Rajputana Infantry.
Red; faced yellow.
Persia, Reshire, Bushire, Koosh-ab.
(2/6th Rajputana Rifles)

21st ByNI (The Marine Battalion)
Raised 1777 as the Marine Battalion.
1903: 121st Pioneers.
Red; faced green.
Persian Gulf, Beni Boo Ali, Burma, Aden, Hyderabad, Punjab, ABYSSINIA.
(1st Bombay Pioneers)

22nd ByNI
Raised 1818 as 2/11th ByNI.
1903: 122nd Rajputana Infantry.
Red; faced dark green, 1882 emerald green.
CHINA 1900.
(3/6th Rajputana Rifles)

23rd ByN Light Infantry
Raised 1820 as 1/12th ByNI.
1889: 23rd Regiment (2nd Battalion Rifle Regiment) Bombay Infantry. 1901: 23rd Bombay Rifles. 1903: 123rd Outram's Rifles.
Red; faced dark green, 1882 emerald green.

1890 Green; faced red.
Kirkee, Persia, AFGHANISTAN 1879–80, BURMA 1885–87.
(4/6th Rajputana Rifles)

24th ByNI
Raised 1820 as 2(Marine)/12th ByNI.
1891: 24th (Baluchistan) Regiment, Bombay Infantry. 1895: 24th (Duchess of Connaught's Own Baluchistan) Regiment, Bombay Infantry. 1903: 124th Duchess of Connaught's Own Baluchistan Infantry.
Red; faced deep green, 1885 emerald green. From 1891 Drab; faced red; red trousers.
Aden, Central India, AFGHANISTAN 1879–80, BRITISH EAST AFRICA 1896.
(1/10th Baluch Regt.)

25th ByN Light Infantry
Raised 1820 as 1st Extra Battalion ByNI.
1889: 25th Regiment (3rd Battalion Rifle Regiment) Bombay Infantry. 1903: 125th Napier's Rifles.
Red; faced pale yellow, 1882 yellow. From 1890 Green; faced red, 1898 scarlet.
Meanee, Hyderabad, Central India, ABYSSINIA, BURMA 1885–87.
(5/6th Rajputana Rifles)

26th ByNI
Raised 1825 as 2nd Extra Battalion ByNI.
1892: 26th (Baluchistan) Regiment Bombay Infantry. 1903: 126th Baluchistan Infantry.
Red; faced light buff, 1884 yellow. 1892 Drab; faced red; red trousers.
Persia, Koosh-ab, CHINA 1900.
(2/10th Baluch Regt.)

27th ByNI or 1st Baluch Regiment
Raised 1844 as the Balooch Battalion or Scinde Baluchi Corps.
1871: 27th Bombay (Light) Infantry or 1st Baluch Regiment. 1888: 27th (1st Baluch Battalion) Bombay Light Infantry. 1903: 127th Baluch Light Infantry. 1909: 127th Princess of Wales's Own Baluch Light Infantry. 1910: 127th Queen Mary's Own Baluch Light Infantry.
Green; faced red; red trousers.
Delhi, ABYSSINIA, AFGHANISTAN 1879–80, BURMA 1885–87, BRITISH EAST AFRICA 1897–99.
(3/10th Baluch Regt.)

28th ByNI
Raised 1846.
1888: 28th (Pioneer) Regiment Bombay Infantry.
1903: 128th Pioneers.
Red; faced pale yellow, 1882 yellow.
KANDAHAR 1880, AFGHANISTAN 1878–80, SUAKIN 1885, TOFREK, PUNJAB FRONTIER, TIRAH.
(3rd Bn. Bombay Pioneers)

29th ByNI or 2nd Baluch Battalion
Raised 1846 as the 2nd Baluch Battalion.
1883: 29th (Duke of Connaught's Own) Bombay Infantry or 2nd Baluch Regiment. 1903: 129th Duke of Connaught's Own Baluchis.
Green; faced red; red trousers.
Persia, Reshire, Bushire, KANDAHAR 1880, AFGHANISTAN 1878–80, EGYPT 1882, TEL-EL-KEBIR.
(4/10th Baluch Regt.)

30th ByNI or Jacob's Rifles
Raised 1858 as 1st Regiment Jacob's Rifles.
1881: 30th ByNI or 3rd Baluch Battalion. 1903: 130th Baluchis. 1906: 130th Prince of Wales's Own Baluchis. 1910: 130th Prince of Wales's Own Baluchis (Jacob's Rifles). 1910: 130th King George's Own Baluchis (Jacob's Rifles).

Left:
Bugler of the 7th (Duke of Connaught's Own) Rajput Regiment at Southampton, 1902. (National Army Museum)

Centre:
Colour-Havildar, 45th Rattray's Sikhs, review order, *c.* 1904. This NCO has the Indian Order of Merit and wears the red kurta, piped white, with a white cummerbund, which replaced the tunic for full dress from 1904 in red- and green-coated regiments. Blue and white turban with steel quoit badge, blue trousers and white gaiters. Watercolour by A. C. Lovett. (National Army Museum)

Right:
Piper, 130th King George's Own Baluchis (Jacob's Rifles) in full dress, 1914. Green turban and tunic, red trousers. Plaid may be Royal Stewart. (Collection R. G. Harris)

1881 Drab. 1883 Green; faced red; red trousers.
AFGHANISTAN 1878–80, CHINA 1900.
(5/10th Baluch Regiment)

The following regiment was raised in 1904 and took the vacant number between the 105th and the 107th:

106th Hazara Pioneers
Drab; faced red.
(1/4th Hazara Pioneers)

Sepoy, 29th Bombay Infantry (2nd Baluch) at Southampton, 1902. (National Army Museum)

Uniforms

In 1855 the British Infantry abolished the old coatee with tails in favour of a tunic with full skirts, which was at first double-breasted but changed to single-breasted a year later. This was a plainer, easier-fitting garment than the coatee and, rather belatedly, followed a trend in military fashion adopted by most European powers in the previous decade. The Indian infantry of the Company's armies continued to wear their version of the coatee, with either dark grey cloth or white linen trousers according to season. Their cumbersome black shakos without peaks had been replaced in the 1840s by the Kilmarnock forage cap, as worn in undress by British infantrymen. European officers in sepoy regiments were dressed similarly to their counterparts in the pre-1855 British Line. As accoutrements the sepoy still had the white cross-belts suspending pouch and bayonet, and, although he had a waist-belt to steady the cross-belts, the British practice of attaching the bayonet to the waist-belt had not yet been adopted. There were also, apart from Gurkhas, rifle companies attached to the red-coated regiments and one Bombay rifle regiment, whose appearance approximated to that of pre-Crimean British riflemen but wearing the Kilmarnock. This was generally the costume of the regular regiments of the three Presidency armies at the outbreak of the Mutiny. The Punjab Irregular Force, first raised as the Frontier Brigade in 1846, were by 1857, with one exception, generally wearing turbans and looser clothing of a khaki colour, following the example of the Corps of Guides, who had been dressed in loose khaki blouses and trousers since they were first raised by Harry Lumsden in 1846. This type of practical clothing was adopted for the new regiments raised in the Punjab during the Mutiny.

After the Mutiny the old coatee uniform was abolished and efforts were made to dress the sepoy more appropriately and with less emphasis on following the fashions of his British counterpart. Initially this went no further than adopting the 1856 tunic, but in 1860 turbans were sanctioned as the sepoy's headdress and gradually, with the lead taken in the Bengal Army, a more 'Indian' type of uniform evolved. In Bengal and Madras this took the form of the so-called 'Zouave' tunic, with a centre panel in the facing colour; but in Bombay a frock, similar to the British infantryman's undress garment, was preferred. All three armies replaced the straight trousers with a 'plus-four' type, worn with gaiters or puttees. Although red continued to predominate in full dress uniforms, the Frontier Force and Punjab regiments stuck to their khaki, or drab as it was officially called, wearing, in full dress, tunics of this colour cut in a more British style, rather than the Zouave type. Green was worn by Rifle regiments and also by the Baluch battalions of the Bombay Army, in the latter case with red trousers. The cut of British officers' dress followed that of the British Line when their regiments were dressed in red, while those of green or drab-coated regiments adopted the dress characteristics of British Rifle regiments. The helmet, covered in white, green, black or drab cloth, replaced the shako as the full dress headgear.

During the Second Afghan War khaki began to be worn in the field by all regiments, and in 1885 was officially authorized for active service. In this dress the sepoy's upper garment was a blouse, or *kurta*, and after 1903 a red or green serge version replaced the tunic for full dress, except in some Frontier Force regiments.

The sepoy's accoutrements broadly followed the current British infantry patterns but with local modifications. They differed chiefly in the use of brown, instead of buff, leather, although some regiments used the latter, and the omission of the knapsack or valise. As firearms developed over the period, the sepoy was always one weapon behind the British infantryman, and it was not until 1914 that he received the most up-to-date rifle.

It is impossible here to consider all the uniform changes and variations of well over a hundred regiments, but the main developments in both full and campaign dress after 1860 can be gleaned from the plate notes and the monotone illustrations, supplemented by the basic uniform details in the preceding section. Readers requiring further details should consult W. Y. Carman's *Indian Army Uniforms—Infantry* (1969).

The Plates

A1 Havildar, 21st Madras Native Infantry, 1861
This NCO wears the 1856 British pattern tunic and trousers introduced for all red-coated Indian infantry to replace the coatee. It was worn by the Madras Army until superseded by the 'Zouave' tunic (see E2) in 1883. The turbans authorized from 1860 were an alternative to the Kilmarnock cap worn previously. Initially in a plain colour of regimental choice, from 1883 they were to be khaki, with a band in the facing colour and a khaki fringe. The ammunition pouch hung behind the right hip and the small pouch on the front of its belt contained caps for the percussion musket.

A2 British Captain, 10th Bengal Native Infantry, c. 1865
The officer is shown in the undress frock worn for daily duties in barracks instead of the 1856 tunic. The frock was of thinner material, had fewer buttons and was less close-fitting than the tunic. It bore no gold lace but had collar and cuffs in the facing colour. The silver star and crown on the collar denote captain's rank, which follows the new rank insignia introduced for the British Army in 1855: colonels and captains sharing the same device, lieutenant-colonels and lieutenants a crown, majors and ensigns a star, field officers being distinguished by extra lace round the tunic collar. He wears the first, officially authorized India-pattern helmet, which had an air-pipe up the back

Lieutenant-Colonel A. P. Elphinstone, 106th Hazara Pioneers, in full dress, 1904. Drab tunic, faced red. (Collection R. G. Harris)

and a *pagri* tied loosely round it. His sword is of the British Army 1822 infantry pattern and is suspended from slings attached to a waist-belt worn under the tunic.

A3 Sepoy, 1st Infantry, Punjab Irregular Force, c. 1865
In the Punjab Irregular Force, only the 1st Infantry (Coke's Rifles) did not wear khaki. It is recorded that their uniform was of drill material, dyed with indigo, as were their turbans, which probably produced a blackish colour, though an early print of the regiment shows the clothing as rifle-green, as it subsequently became, and the turbans as dark blue. The same print (see monotone illustrations) gives the officers and NCOs turbans in which red, blue and yellow predominate. The front of the tunic was fastened with concealed buttons. Native shoes were worn and the brown leather accoutrements of waist- and pouch-belts included a cap pouch to the right of the waist clasp, and a hammer to assist in ramming the ball down the rifled barrel of the firearm, probably the Brunswick rifle. A

Sword bayonet was issued with this weapon. The 1st Infantry distinguished themselves on the Umbeyla Expedition of 1863 but suffered heavy casualties, perhaps due to the conspicuousness of the dark uniforms against the dun-coloured hills.

B1 Sepoy, 15th Punjab Infantry, 1860
This figure is based on a photograph taken during the China War of 1860 of this regiment, which was renumbered 23rd in 1861. It shows the typical khaki clothing with long-skirted tunic, worn by the Punjab regiments raised during the Mutiny. In addition to the main ammunition pouch hanging at the rear, another pouch of similar design, but smaller, was fastened to the waist-belt to give easier access when loading. A cap pouch was sewn into the tunic just above the waist. The Indian officers carried native swords, or *tulwars*, suspended from a brown leather waist-belt with large rectangular buckle. Sepoys wore native shoes when in India, but boots were normally issued to regiments on foreign service.

B2 Sepoy, 27th Bombay Native Infantry (1st Baluch Regiment), 1868
This regiment (and that in B1) formed part of the expedition to Abyssinia in 1868 and a photograph taken in the field shows them in the costume depicted. The red-laced, dark green tunics were peculiar to the Baluch battalions, as were the red trousers which had been worn since 1851. For a time in the early 1860s green trousers were ordered for British officers, though how long this ruling lasted and whether it applied to all ranks is uncertain; red was the colour for all by the 1880s. In the late 'seventies the Baluch sepoys adopted a plain green frock of the Bombay pattern (see C1) with red facings. The accoutrements here follow the general pattern of the period, with the large pouch behind and a cap pouch on the waist-belt. A British officer described the Baluchis as 'such strange wild-looking fellows' and hoped they were 'plucky and ferocious'.

B3 Sepoy, 3rd Sikh Infantry, Punjab Irregular Force, 1863
This figure is from a photograph taken during the Umbeyla campaign of 1863 on the North-West Frontier. Apart from the large Sikh khaki turban

with orange fringe as worn by this regiment, his clothing and accoutrements are similar to those in B1 above, though the tunic has yellow facings then worn by the 3rd Sikhs (later black) and native shoes are in use. Over the tunic he wears a *poshteen*, the sheepskin coat with fleece inside, frequently worn on the Frontier instead of a greatcoat. He is armed with a short rifle instead of a musket. This costume was far more suitable for frontier operations than the red frocks worn by the British infantry in this campaign.

C1 Naik, 1st or Grenadier Regiment, Bombay Native Infantry, c. 1880
The Bombay sepoy's full dress tunic, or frock, which replaced the 1856 British tunic in about 1880, is depicted here. The facing colour appears only on the collar and shoulder-straps. It was only worn by the Bombay infantry. The 1st Bombay Infantry, as Grenadiers, had the distinction of a grenade on the collar. The leather binding to the white gaiters was another peculiarity of the Bombay regiments. This figure is in review order and wears a pipe-clayed waist-belt with a black leather pouch, as in the British infantry, in contrast to the brown leather more customarily seen in the Bengal and Madras infantry. When the British infantry received the Martini-Henry rifle in the mid-1870s, their Snider-Enfields, depicted here, were turned over to the Indian troops. The Snider was the first breech-loader used by Indian infantry.

C2 British Lieutenant, 6th Infantry, Punjab Frontier Force, c. 1885
This shows the British Rifles style of tunic, fastened with cord loops and olivets, worn by British officers of Frontier Force and other non-red-coated regiments in full dress. The collar and cuffs in the regimental facing colour were decorated with varying arrangements of braid according to rank. From 1880 the rank badges were placed on the shoulder cords and were: colonel, crown and two stars; lieutenant-colonel, crown and star; major, crown; captain, two stars; lieutenant, one star; second lieutenant, no badge. The full dress head-gear was the cloth-covered helmet of the type which had replaced the air-pipe version about 1870, complete with white metal spike, badge, chin-chain and binding. The badge worn

on helmet and pouch-belt by the 6th Infantry was a plain Maltese Cross with the numeral 'VI' in the centre, and the topmost fold of their red pagris was drab. This regiment was unique in having black leather belt and slings, other drab-uniformed regiments having brown.

C3 Bugle-Major, 1st Sikh Infantry, Punjab Frontier Force, c. 1880

This figure wears the full dress uniform of a senior NCO of a Frontier Force regiment, the 1st Sikhs, with yellow facings. The tunic was cloth but the trousers, which were cut very full, were of cotton drill, while the buttoned gaiters were of canvas. The sandals were usually worn over bare feet but socks were issued for the cold weather. This NCO wears the Indian Mutiny medal.

D1 Sepoy, 45th (Rattray's Sikh) Regiment, Bengal Native Infantry, 1879

This uniform is taken from a photograph of the 45th Sikhs in the Second Afghan War and is typical of the half-khaki, half-peacetime dress worn by

both British and Indian regiments in the early stages of this campaign. A khaki kurta has replaced the red tunic but is worn with the full dress trousers, which are tucked into khaki puttees with the man's socks pulled up over them. This regiment had the modified Indian version of the British infantry's valise pattern equipment with only one pouch and the ball bag and no valise, but many Indian regiments (and some British) still had the old pouch-belt accoutrements in this war. The new equipment was eventually issued in a brown leather version to all sepoy regiments. A greatcoat or blanket is strapped to this man's back, and a haversack and water-bottle complete his equipment.

D2 British Officer, 5th Infantry, Punjab Frontier Force, 1880

This figure, taken from a photograph, shows the campaign dress of an officer in the Second Afghan War. He wears an undress frock with regimental facings and a plain helmet, the costume making an austere contrast with the full dress in C2. Puttees were usually worn but this officer is shown in British infantry marching gaiters, which curiously were seldom, if ever, worn in India by British regiments. His sword and revolver are supported by a Sam Browne belt, which first enjoyed wide popularity in this campaign.

D3 Sepoy, 23rd (Punjab) Regiment, Bengal Native Infantry (Pioneers), 1880

Another Afghan War figure; his clothing is all khaki except the turban. The Pioneer battalions had special equipment to carry their picks or spades, this man's spade blade being contained in the satchel on his back. As Pioneers also had to fight as infantry, he has two ammunition pouches pushed round on the belt to the rear. A blanket was sometimes carried rolled between the satchel and the man's back.

E1 Sepoy, 26th Punjab Regiment, Bengal Infantry, 1896

An Afridi sepoy in drab full dress, similar to that worn by the Frontier Force. Note how the puttees are worn inside the boots at this date. The Martini-Henry rifle has now replaced the Snider, British troops having received the Lee-Metford.

E2 Havildar, 15th Bengal Infantry (Ludhiana Sikhs), 1898

This figure shows the so-called 'Zouave' tunic, introduced for red-coated Bengal regiments in the late 1860s and in Madras from 1883. Initially the centre panel in the facing colour sloped diagonally down from the waist, but from the late nineties it was square-cut. This tunic was worn by all Indian ranks, but not by British officers, whose tunics were of the British Line pattern. The turban is now more neatly tied and bears the steel quoit of the Sikhs. The havildar's medals are: Egyptian Medal (for the Sudan 1885), Indian General Service Medal, India Medal, and Khedive of Egypt's Star.

E3 British Major, 29th (Duke of Connaught's Own) Bombay Infantry (2nd Baluch Regiment), 1896

By this date officers of the 'green' Baluch regiments (27th, 29th, 30th), as opposed to the drab-coated 24th and 26th, had tunics virtually identical to the British 60th Rifles. All five regiments had red breeches or trousers. Compare the major's collar and cuff braiding for this type of tunic with the lieutenant's in C2. An Indian officer and sepoys of this regiment can be found among the monotone illustrations. The brown pouch-belt and slings contrast rather unfavourably with the Rifles-type tunic. The officer's medals are: Second Afghan War, Kabul to Kandahar Star 1880, Egyptian Medal and Khedive's Star for the 1882 campaign.

F1 Sepoy, 1st Madras Pioneers, 1886

This regiment took part in the Burma War of 1885–87 dressed thus, though puttees may have replaced the gaiters shown here. His pioneer equipment is similar to that in D3 but he carries a pick-head in a leather cover and wears his pouches in front. His rifle is still the Snider and he carries his greatcoat in a roll. The regiment's full dress can be found among the monotone illustrations.

F2 Sepoy, 36th (Sikh) Regiment, Bengal Infantry, 1897

This sepoy is dressed as for the Tirah campaign of 1897. He wears a poshteen over his khaki kurta and, though on service, has his quoit over his turban. The equipment is now the Indian version of the Slade-Wallace pattern. The haversack and water-bottle straps are of equal width, the latter being round and covered with khaki cloth. This was the regiment that held Fort Gulistan (see 'On Campaign' section).

F3 Havildar, The Queen's Own Corps of Guides (Infantry), Punjab Frontier Force, 1897

This Afridi NCO is dressed and equipped similarly to the Sikh above, but carries his poshteen strapped to his equipment and wears nailed sandals instead of boots. The Guides took part in the relief of Chitral (see 'On Campaign') and the Malakand expedition of 1897 wearing this type of kit.

G1 Havildar, 125th Napier's Rifles, c. 1905

After the Kitchener reforms of 1903 red- and green-coated infantry adopted a serge kurta instead of the

tunic or frock for full dress, with piping and cummerbund in the facing colour. The 125th had worn rifle-green since 1890 and, as a Rifle regiment, wore puttees rather than white gaiters. Its Indian officers wore a black-buttoned tunic with black pouch-belt and waist-belt. Sepoys now had the 1895 pattern Lee-Enfield rifle. The silver whistle attached to the kurta was a havildar's distinction, like those on the officers' pouch-belts.

G2 Subadar, 16th Rajputs (The Lucknow Regiment), c. 1905

When the full dress serge kurtas were introduced for sepoys, they were also worn in some regiments by Indian officers, but others adopted a tunic similar to the British officers', as shown here. The officer's sash was now worn round the waist. The short white gaiters over blue puttees seem to have been peculiar to the 16th's Indian officers, most regiments retaining the long white gaiters. Until 1888 Indian officers' rank badges had been worn just below the collar on the right side: gold crown for the subadar-major, gold crossed swords for subadars, single gold sword for jemadars. These changed to silver embroidered badges worn on the shoulder straps: a crown, two stars, and a single star respectively.

British officers had changed by this date to the Wolseley pattern helmet, with similar embellishments in full dress as worn on the previous pattern.

G3 Naik, 57th Wilde's Rifles (Frontier Force), 1914

Drab-uniformed regiments did not assume the

Group of officers attending the Coronation of 1902. *Left to right, back row:* 15th Sikhs, 23rd Punjab Pioneers, 38th Dogras, 3rd Bombay Light Infantry, 1st Infantry Hyderabad Contingent, 1st Madras Pioneers, 32nd Burma Infantry, 1st Sikhs FF (?), 20th Punjabis, 20th Madras Infantry, 10th Jats, Mharwara Battalion. *Centre row:* 15th Sikhs (undress), Bombay Sappers & Miners, 2nd Bombay Grenadiers, 32nd Burma Infantry, not known, 29th Bombay (2nd Baluch). *Front row:* 1st Bombay Grenadiers, 39th Garhwal Rifles, 1st Punjab Infantry FF, 1st Brahman Infantry, 7th Rajputs, 33rd Punjabis, 24th Bombay (Baluch). (Collection R. G. Harris)

kurta for full dress but retained their tunics with regimental facings. The waist-belt now had a plain brass buckle and in review order, as here, four ten-round pouches from the 1903 Bandolier Equipment (see H2) were worn on it. The naik's medal is for China 1900. By 1914 Indian infantry at last received the same weapon as their British comrades—the Short Lee-Enfield, 1902 pattern.

H1 Jemadar, 14th Bengal Infantry (Ferozepore Sikhs), 1900

This jemadar is dressed in the service kit worn when leaving India for the Boxer Rebellion in China. Both British and Indian officers of the 14th Sikhs wore the turban and quoit in this dress, but the former had khaki drill tunics, breeches and puttees instead of the kurta, loose trousers and gaiters worn by the jemadar. His accoutrements include re-volver holster, binocular case, haversack and water-bottle. Note that his belt is different from the Sam Browne worn by British officers.

H2 Sepoy, 41st Dogras, c. 1910

This figure shows the sepoy's field service kit just prior to the Great War. The khaki turban with regimental fringe, kurta, trousers, puttees and boots are worn with the 1903 Bandolier Equipment. This consisted of a fifty-round leather bandolier, four extra pouches on the belt, haversack and water-bottle, with blanket and groundsheet strapped at the rear.

H3 Lance-Naik, 39th Garhwal Rifles, 1914

This NCO is dressed in the kit worn by this regiment when it left India for France in 1914. Before going into the trenches in late October the men were issued with British khaki serge service dress but retained their slouch hats. In full dress the Garhwalis wore the black Kilmarnock and rifle-green tunic, trousers and black puttees of the Gurkhas and followed the latter's service dress, adopted from 1903, of hat, khaki drill tunic, shorts, hose-tops and puttees. Indian troops in France fought in the 1903 equipment. The second v.c. won by an Indian soldier was awarded to Naik Darwan Sing Negi of the Garhwalis for gallantry on 23 November 1914.

Notes sur les planches en couleur

A1 Le port de la tunique de coupe britannique était de rigueur dans l'armée de Madras de 1856 à 1883. Le turban remplaça le 'Kilmarnock' en 1860. La cartouchière pend derrière la hanche droite, et la petite poche située sur le devant de la bandoulière contient les amorces à mousquet. **A2** La *undress frock* se portait pour le service intérieur journalier, au lieu de la tunique de 1856. L'étoile et la couronne d'argent sur le parement du col aux couleurs du régiment désignent le rang de capitaine. **A3** Tous les autres régiments de la Punjab Irregular Force portaient l'uniforme khaki; le 1st Infantry portait 'le treillis'—de ton neutre—teint à l'indigo.

B1 Cette illustration s'inspire d'une photographie prise au cours de la guerre de Chine de 1860; elle nous montre la tenue typique des régiments pendant la Mutinerie. **B2** L'uniforme rouge et vert foncé était le propre des bataillons baloutchis, vus ici en Abyssinie en 1868. **B3** Reconstitué d'après une photographie de la Campagne d'Umbeyla en 1863, ce costume, que complète la capote *poshteen*, est la tenue des campagnes d'hiver de la frontière Nord-Ouest.

C1 L'uniforme de parade de l'infanterie de Bombay, qui fut mis en usage vers 1880. L'écusson grenade au col était particulier au 1st BNI. **C2** La tenue de parade des officiers britanniques de la Frontier Force était de style semblable à celui des régiments de Rifles. **C3** Grande tenue d'officier supérieur de la Frontier Force.

D1 Uniforme typique—mi-khaki, mi-cérémonie—des débuts de la seconde Guerre afghane, en 1879. **D2** L'austère tenue de Campagne de la seconde Guerre afghane, en contraste avec la grande tenue aux vives couleurs, de l'illustration C2. **D3** Tenue de combat typique de la fin de la seconde Guerre afghane, avec équipement pionnier en plus.

E1 Un Afridi *sepoy* en uniforme de cérémonie 'drab' semblable à celui que portaient les unités des Forces-frontière. **E2** La soi-disant tunique 'Zouave' que portaient les régiments à capotes rouges du Bengal à partir de 1860, de même que les unités de Madras à partir de 1883. Noter le palet d'acier, emblème de sa religion, sur le turban de ce Sikh. **E3** Officiers des 'Balouchs Verts'—les 27è 29è et 30è de la Bombay Infantry—portaient alors des uniformes presqu'identiques à ceux des 60th Rifles britanniques.

F1 Tenue de campagne que portait ce régiment pendant la Guerre de Birmanie, 1885-87. **F2** L'un des héros de Fort Gulistan pendant la Campagne de Tyrah en 1897, en tenue de combat d'hiver avec *poshteen*. **F3** Uniforme porté par un NCO Afridi au cours des campagnes du Chitral et de Malakand.

G1 Le *kurta*, qui fit son apparition en 1903, avec passepoil et ceinture aux couleurs du régiment. **G2** Après 1903 certains officiers hindous adoptèrent également le *kurta*; d'autres portaient une tunique dans le style britannique, comme celle-ci. **G3** Les régiments qui portaient l'uniforme *drab* n'adoptèrent pas le *kurta*; ils continuèrent à porter la tunique à parements aux couleurs du régiment.

H1 Uniforme porté par les officiers hindous de ce régiment au cours de la Boxer Rebellion de Chine, en 1900. **H2** Uniforme de campagne typique de l'époque qui précéda la Première Guerre Mondiale. **H3** Uniforme porté par ce régiment lors du départ pour la France, en 1914. Une fois en France, les hommes furent équipés d'uniformes britanniques de serge khaki, mais ils conservèrent le couvre-chef caractéristique.

Farbtafeln

A1 Waffenröcke vom britischen Muster wurden zwischen den Jahren 1856 und 1883 von den Soldaten des Madrasheeres getragen. Die 'Kilmarnock'-Mütze wurde durch den Turban ersetzt. Die Patronentasche hängt hinter der linken Hüfte und der kleine Beutel vorne am Kreuzgurt enthält Zündhütchen für die Flinte. **A2** Der *undress frock* (Interimsrock) wurde statt dem 1856er Waffenrock beim täglichen Kasernendienst getragen. Hauptmannsrang wird durch den silbernen Stern und die Krone am regimentsaufschlagfärbigen Kragen gekennzeichnet. **A3** Alle andere Regimente des Punjab Irregular Force trugen khaki-färbige Uniforme; das 1st Infantry war in neutralfärbigem, mit indigo gefärbtem Drillich gekleidet.

B1 Diese Abbildung ist nach einem im 1860er chinesischen Kriege aufgenommenen Photo nachgemacht worden und stellt typische Figuren der nach der Meuterei ausgehobenen Pandschabiregimente dar. **B2** Die dunkelgrün und rote Uniform war den Baluchbataillonen eigen, die hier im Jahre 1868 beim abyssinischen Feldzuge geschildert sind. **B3** Nach einem Photo des Umbeylafeldzuges im Jahre 1863, diese Abbildung stellt sie typische Feldzugsuniform, einschliesslich *poshteen*—(Schaffel)—Mantel dar, die beim Winterkämpfen an der Nordwestgrenze getragen wurde.

C1 Die Paradeuniform der Bombayinfanterie, die c. 1880 im Gebrauch eingetreten ist. Die Regimentsaufschlagfarbe ist nur am Kragen und an den Achselklappen eigen. Das Granatemblem am Kragen war dem 1st BNI eigen. **C2** Die Galauniform der britischen Offiziere des Frontier Force war nach jener der Rifle Regimente gestaltet. **C3** Galauniform eines dienstälteren Unteroffiziers des Frontier Force.

D1 Typische Uniform—halb khaki, halb Paradeuniform—die in den früheren Stadien des 2. Afghankrieges, 1879, getragen wurde. **D2** Die ungezierte Feldzugsuniform des 2. Afghankrieges im Gegensatz zur farbenfreudigen, in C2 abgebildeten Paradeuniform. **D3** Typische Feldzugsuniform der späteren Stadien des 2. Afghankrieges, mit zusätzlicher Pionierausrüstung.

E1 Afridi *sepoy* im *drab* Paradeuniform, den von den Frontier Force-Einheiten getragenen Uniformen ähnlich. **E2** Der sogenannte 'Zouave' Waffenrock ab den späteren 60erjahren von den in rot angezogenen Bengalregimenten und ab 1883 von den Madraseinheiten getragen. Bemerkenswert ist es, dass dieser Sikh die Stahlwurfscheibe seiner Religion auf seinem Turban trägt. **E3** Offiziere der 'Grünen Baluchen'—die 27., 29. und 30. Bombay Infantry—trugen zu dieser Zeit Uniforme, die jener der 60th Rifles fast identisch waren.

F1 Feldzugsuniform von diesem Regiment im Burmakriege von 1885-87 getragen. **F2** Einer der Fort Gulistanhelde im Tyrahfeldzuge 1897 im Winterfeldzugsuniform mit *poshteen* dargestellt. **F3** Uniform von einem Afridi-Unteroffizier während der Chitral und Malakandfeldzüge getragen.

G1 Der im Jahre 1903 eingeführte *kurta* mit Schnurbesatz und Leibbinde von der Regimentsaufschlagfarbe. **G2** Ab 1903 haben sich etliche indische Offiziere den *kurta* auch angeeignet; andere, wie hier abgebildet, trugen einen Waffenrock britischer Art. **G3** Regimente, die *drab* Uniforme trugen haben sich den *kurta* nicht angeeignet, sondern behielten ihre Waffenröcke mit Aufschlägen aus der Regimentsfarbe.

H1 Uniform von indischen Offizieren dieses Regiments im Jahre 1900 während der Boxer Rebellion in China getragen. **H2** Typische Feldzugsuniform von der Zeit kurz vor dem ersten Weltkriege. **H3** Uniform von diesem Regiment zur Zeit der Einschiffung nach Frankreich im Jahre 1914. In Frankreich wurden die Soldaten mit der britischen khaki-Sergeuniform ausgestattet, behielten, aber, ihre charakteristischen Hüte.